THE SPIRIT BADE ME GO

The Spirit Bade Me Go

The Astounding Move of God
in the Denominational Churches

by

David J. du Plessis

LOGOS INTERNATIONAL
Plainfield, N.J. 07060

———————

Logos — Fountain Trust
Central Hall, Durnsford Road
London SW 19, G.B.

Published by special arrangement
with David J. du Plessis

Revised Edition

Copyright 1970   By
LOGOS INTERNATIONAL
Plainfield, N.J.

ISBN 0-912106-59-X

Printed in the United States of America

CONTENTS

FOREWORD

The Lord has given my old friend, David J. du Plessis, an exceptional ministry in recent years, helping those who have believed through grace (Acts 18:27) in the matter of receiving the enduement of power from on high by the baptism in the Holy Spirit as promised by the risen Christ.

For half a century this particular testimony has been almost exclusively restricted to what has been known as the Pentecostal Movement. Therein millions have received a personal Pentecostal experience. Now it is cause for great joy that many more within the older denominations of the Church are also pressing into this blessing. They are not sharing in a movement but in a *revival*.

David du Plessis has won hearts everywhere by his frank demeanor and his gifted opening of the Scriptures. He has mixed freely in circles formerly doubtful of nominally Pentecostal preachers. He has won their confidence without compromising in any way his own personal testimony of what the Lord has done for him in the things of the Spirit. He fully merits the confidence shown to him. He is not the official agent of any movement or denomination but acts only as a servant of the living God.

Some of his messages have been especially blessed to hearts hungry for the Promise of the Father; and whether we agree with every detail of exposition or not, we wish them a wide ministry through the printed page.

In 1952, in a tribute to my friend, I wrote these words: Such work "requires God's man, with God's gifts and God's burden for God's work for God's glory." Now, nearly ten years later, I find no reason to change these words.

Donald Gee
Editor of *Pentecost*

Kenley, Surrey
England

TESTIMONY OF A REFORMED
CHURCH MINISTER

I am deeply concerned over the statements in recent publications regarding the ministry of the Rev. David J. du Plessis. I am particularly disturbed by the accusation that he has claimed or attempted to speak for the Pentecostals. I am completely at a loss to understand how anyone who has heard him could get such an impression. I have heard him a great many times. I heard him speak to a group of ministers and professors in my own church. I heard him address the students at Yale Divinity School. I have listened to him explaining the Pentecostal experience and its Scriptural foundations to ordinary church members. I have also been present in small group discussions in which I participated. At no time have I heard him say that he was speaking for any movement or that he was representing any movement. In fact, he leaned over backward to give the opposite impression. He seemed rather anxious to make it clear that he was giving his own testimony, and that he was ministering on those occasions and in those circumstances because "the Spirit bade him go." I always felt that he represented an experience rather than a movement.

Then with great ability and loyalty I heard him defend the Movement when he was questioned about some of its practices and teachings. Only when he was asked whether he was actually a minister of the Movement did he say that he held papers with the Assemblies of God, for which he expressed a profound regard. When questioned about the World Conference, he would point out that this was not an organization, and that he was honorary secretary with no authority, only with more knowledge about the Movement than most other leaders may have because it was his privilege to serve almost all the Pentecostal movements in the world. I think he made it very clear that he was not seeking recognition of the Pentecostal Movement, but rather of the work of the Holy Spirit in and through this movement in the world.

To those of us who have been blessed with the baptism in the Holy Spirit and who are still ministering in the pulpits of the historic churches, his ministry has been a rich blessing. He has encouraged us to be true to our testimony and yet serve the Church faithfully by graciously and wisely bringing the truth of a Pentecostal experience to them.

I, together with many of my colleagues and ministers in the Episcopalian, Presbyterian, Methodist, and other confessions, have come to look upon David du Plessis as the dauntless champion of the truth of the doctrine and experience of the Pentecostal blessing. In our churches he has been able to testify before those at levels which we never contact. His ministry has eliminated the opposition of our leaders to the Pentecostal experience with the confirmation of "speaking with tongues."

Only those of us who serve and fellowship in churches that are members of the National Council and The World Council of Churches can appreciate this man's ministry when we see and feel the strong "wind of the Spirit" which is bringing a change of spiritual climate into the councils of the historic churches.

We know of no other Pentecostal minister who has shown such keen and capable leadership in bringing, without compromise, the message and experience of the Holy Spirit into circles and at levels where many thought it impossible. It must be clear that he has wasted no time and effort in attacking the churches but has faithfully, humbly, and effectively presented and preached a positive and powerful Gospel. For this we love him and respect him highly. I know of no one of whom I can more definitely say, "Here is a man raised up by God for a specific mission."

Harald Bredesen, Pastor

Reformed Church
Mount Vernon, N.Y.

TESTIMONY OF A BAPTIST
CHURCH MINISTER

In November of 1959 I first met Brother David at Princeton Seminary where he had been invited to be the missions speaker that year. Subsequently I have been in several interdenominational meetings with him. Each meeting has but served to increase my Christian love for the man and to deepen my appreciation for his ministry among denominational ministers and their churches. Never have I heard him, even by implication, profess to represent anything or anyone other than the experience of the baptism in the Holy Spirit. Unflinchingly and forthrightly he has faced the most searching questions relating to the practices and teachings of the Pentecostal movements. Kindly yet forthrightly he has wholeheartedly championed the Pentecostal Movement. His attitude towards his Pentecostal brethren has always been, in my presence, affectionately loyal to them. His witness to the reality of the baptism in the Holy Spirit is always gracious but uncompromising. In my humble opinion, he merits not the censure but the wholehearted confidence and support of every Spirit-filled believer in these last days.

Perhaps you will better appreciate my interest in this matter when I say that Brother David's ministry to me has been most graciously blessed of God, culminating in my own experience of the baptism in the Holy Spirit, and I thank God for David's part in helping to lead me into it. I know of no other man who is being used so effectively of God to reach the denominational people and ministers with this precious truth. I know by personal experience. Brother du Plessis' teaching and example have taught me a new appreciation and respect for my own denominational heritage, while maintaining my allegiance to the experience of the baptism in the Holy Spirit.

I pray that when you read Brother du Plessis' testimony, you will arrive at the same conclusion as the Jerusalem presbytery that examined Peter concerning his ministry to the Gentile centurion, Cornelius: "When they heard these things, they held their peace and glorified God" (Acts 11:18).

Howard Ervin, Pastor

Emmanuel Baptist Church
Atlantic Highlands, N.J.

INTRODUCTION

This book really "just happened." Most of the material came from talks and lectures given without script or notes as the Holy Spirit gave or manifested the Word. These messages were tape-recorded and afterwards transcribed. In a sense, then, it was my privilege to edit and prepare for publication in this form those revelations that I received from Him while ministering in conferences, councils, institutions, and churches.

I have tried to collect material that would supply the most information and teaching. If the reader should find any repetition, it is because the same thoughts were given in several different gatherings. I sought to keep everything true to fact, and report "just as it happened."

On numerous occasions—in conferences, retreats, advances, and regular church services—friends have pleaded with me to put into print the things I have said, or rather those things that the Holy Spirit has said through me. To attempt to write about those things would not be quite the same as quoting more directly the utterances made under the unction of the Spirit.

I realize that the message might have been for a certain group, or class, or council, but I am sure we can all learn from what the Spirit has had to say to others. I trust, therefore, that my friends will not expect a story that is chronologically arranged, nor messages that are homiletically developed. At all times I am far more concerned about the power of the Gospel than the mechanics of preaching. Like Paul, I ministered "in weakness, and in fear, and in much trembling. And my speech and my preaching was not with enticing words of man's wisdom, but in demonstration of the Spirit and of power: that your faith should not stand in the wisdom of men, but in the power of God" (I Cor. 2:3–5).

7

A PENTECOSTAL IN
ECUMENICAL CIRCLES

A lecture given at Highleigh, Hoddesdon, Herts, England

What is a "pentecostalist"? It is someone who can testify to having enjoyed the very same experience as that which the Apostles of our Lord had on the day of Pentecost according to Acts 2. I hear the term "pentecostal" more frequently than "pentecostalist," so I shall make use of the former term in this message.

What is the Pentecostal Movement? On the whole this term includes all those societies and movements or missions which teach and preach that all Christians should receive the baptism in the Holy Spirit as they did on the day of Pentecost according to Acts 2:4, with the evidence of speaking with other tongues as the Spirit gives utterance. This seemed to be the "proof" of the baptism in the Spirit that the Apostles recognized.

In Acts 10:45, 46, St. Luke says: "On the Gentiles also was poured out the gift of the Holy Ghost. *For* they heard them speak with tongues, and magnify God." The phenomenon of tongues appeared again in Bible schools and in missions and prayer groups at the turn of the century. Today there are scores of societies, often referred to as sects, that have tens of thousands of churches in every part of the world, with millions of members who have actually received the baptism in the Holy Spirit and have spoken with tongues. The entire Pentecostal Movement has about ten million adherents and is one of the fastest growing, fundamentally Christian movements in the world.

In 1900 when this new revival began, there was a battle against it at once. The opposition was not so much against the teaching of the baptism in the Spirit as against the speaking with tongues. All the historic churches rejected this vehemently. It was considered rank heresy to claim to speak with tongues by the Spirit. But *now*, after fifty years, the climate has changed. Today the same phenomenon of tongues is being witnessed in many of the historic churches. Last year American papers carried headlines like these: "Strange Manifestations—Speaking with Tongues Amazing Churches Again" and "Staid Episcopal Clergyman Speaking with Tongues." This partly gives you the reason why a radical Pentecostal like myself has become involved in ecumenical activities.

I was born in South Africa and came from French Huguenot stock. Then I was born-again in 1916. Actually I was a little white heathen saved by the life and ministry of black Christians. My father was building a home for missionaries in Basotuland, and that was when and where it happened.

The impact upon my young life was not from the preaching of the Gospel, but rather the miracle of the change that I saw in the lives of illiterate pagans around me. What Christ did for them and what the Holy Spirit did through them deeply impressed me. I knew that I had nothing of that. I realized that it was not literacy that changed them, for they had none. I knew their testimonies were not intellectual, for there was too much evidence of the supernatural. I knew it was divine, for many of these people had been steeped in witchcraft and demonism, and now they were completely delivered and changed into saints who loved Jesus so much that they would die for Him.

In 1918 when we had moved back to the Union of South Africa, I was in high school. Then I began to seek the same blessing and the Lord graciously met me and baptized me as He had baptized the saints in New Testament churches according to the book of Acts. So, I am an old-timer in Pentecost and I have seen great miracles during the past forty-three years.

I now realize that what the churches need today is this blessing. Recently Dr. Carl Henry, editor of *Christianity Today,* wrote: "In twentieth-century Christianity the Holy Spirit is still a *displaced person.* Liberal theology exiled this divine person from the life of the Church in favor of simply divine 'function.' Recently a distinguished theologian told me: 'When Christianity lost the Holy Spirit as the divine person who leads into all truth, the Spirit was soon misunderstood (by idealistic philosophy) only as Mind, indeed as human mind. The ability of distinguishing spirits was lost. How right he was. Whenever the Church makes the Spirit of God a refugee, the Church—not the Spirit—becomes the vagabond."

Almost everywhere I go I hear of the lack of the Holy Spirit and His life in the churches. People have lost interest in church services because there is so little of relevancy to their spiritual problems to be found there. Man's spirit hungers after God. Only the Holy Spirit is the water of life that will quench the thirst of the human soul.

Then I think of what Dr. John A. Mackay, immediate past president of both Princeton Theological Seminary and the Presbyterian Alliance, recently told a Presbyterian convention: "A crudely emotional approach to religion is preferable to religious formalism which is purely aesthetic and orderly and lacking in dynamic power." He said further: "One of our serious troubles in the Church today is that it has become legitimate to be emotional in anything but religion. The need is for something that will summon one's whole enthusiasm. The moment the Church becomes completely programized and de-personalized, it becomes a monument to God's memory and not an instrument of His living power."

Statements like these from ecclesiastical leaders and theologians disturb me, because these are confessions that they realize something is wrong with the Church. Something is lacking, but confession is not enough; there must be an acceptance of God's remedy—a Pentecostal revival in the churches.

I began preaching at a very youthful age. In those days there was much preaching against the Pentecostals. I used to listen to Dutch Reformed ministers preach against us and call us false prophets standing on street corners. Then I would promptly go back to the street corner and preach against "these blind leaders of the blind." How we attacked one another. But I thought it was my duty to "contend for the faith."

My parents had been turned out of the Dutch Reformed Church, and I had great bitterness in my heart for this injustice to people who lived like saints. Yes, I could quote Scripture that would sometimes seem to cool off the heat of my bitterness. I remember one day I was challenged to "speak with tongues." I said: "I certainly will not." "But why not?" Quick on the trigger I said: "Because the Bible says: 'Cast not your pearls before swine.'" How good I felt that I could call them "swine." Later

I discovered this was not "in the Spirit" but very much in the flesh. I was still so carnal.

Do I hear you say: "But the Spirit should make you perfect"? Yes, He does. But He does it by manifesting himself through imperfect people. The Church at Corinth was one of the most carnal churches, yet they had more manifestations than others. If you ask me why, I would say: "Because the Holy Spirit sought so desperately to wake them up. He is as faithful to plead with us to repent as to convict us of our faults."

In 1947 the first World Conference of Pentecostal churches was called in Zurich, Switzerland. They gathered from many countries and I came from South Africa. The conference took no real decision for further conferences, so in 1948 the leading brethren asked me to convene the next conference in 1949 in Paris, France. Thus up to 1958 I served most of the time in what some now call the capacity of ecumenical secretary of the Movement.

I have just returned from the sixth Pentecostal World Conference in Jerusalem. How good it was to be there without administrative responsibilities. The Israeli Government had loaned their great new convention hall to us for the weekend of May 19 to 21. I shall never forget that great Communion service on Sunday morning when about 3,000 delegates and visitors from 40 countries sat down at the table of the Lord.

Let me explain. Even though we have a world conference now, the Pentecostal Movement had never been developed or propagated from one center, unless that center is heaven. I do not think there will ever be one central world headquarters. This revival "just happened" in most countries and has become indigenous almost everywhere. There is no man who can claim to have been the founder of this movement. It is the work of the Holy Spirit. When we first met in 1947 there developed better understanding, more recognition, and more appreciation of one another as leaders. We were all happy to recognize that the Lord was bringing His people together. My personal ambition was to see the entire movement united on the basis of recognition rather than by organization. We do have a lot of divisions on issues of doctrine and church government, just like many other great Protestant movements

When the Protestants came together in 1948 to form the World Council of Churches at the first Assembly in Amsterdam, I heard it said: "This is the work of the devil. This is an attempt to form a super-church." I was greatly puzzled, for I could not believe that God would allow the Protestant world to become an instrument of the devil. Why should Pentecostal unity be of the Lord and Protestant unity be of the devil? Was it not the Lord who was moving us to unity in both movements? These questions kept troubling me until I began to pray earnestly about *His* purposes.

In 1951 the Lord spoke to me and clearly told me to go and witness to the leaders of the World Council of Churches. In my prayers I said: "Lord, I have preached so much against them. What do I say to them now? They will not listen to me. Their churches have put our people out of their fellowship. That is why we have now a separate Pentecostal Movement. The churches were not willing to listen to the testimony of those who speak with tongues." But the Lord kept telling me to go and witness to them.

Besides speaking with tongues, there was another very important doctrine and practice which the churches had rejected— namely, divine healing. In my estimation Mr. James Moor Hickson was the man God used to really set the churches right on this matter. Pentecostals could not do it, although they were preaching the message and praying for the sick in almost every meeting in those days. Till this day I consider Mr. Hickson as God's great apostle to restore to the world the reality of divine healing.

Finally I decided to obey the Lord. I asked my wife to prepare an early breakfast because I was going to New York that day. She asked me what I was going to do. I explained that the Lord had commissioned me to go and witness to the leaders of the World Council of Churches. I can still hear her saying, "What will you try next?" I replied: "I am not trying anything, I am just obeying the Lord. But I will be back by lunch." I expected to be dismissed so quickly that I would not want to stay in New York very long. At that time I lived close by in Connecticut.

When the offices on Fifth Avenue opened I was there. I announced myself and made sure there was no mistake about who and what I was—a Pentecostal, and one of the worst, actually the world secretary. In the train on my way in I had decided to make things so hot that those I spoke to would have no trouble in knowing what I had to say, and I expected them to object and reject. But the hotter I made it the better my friends seemed to like it. This one friend kept saying: "Go on, tell us some more. We have been waiting for a fellow like you to come and talk to us." This continued until lunchtime. I apologized for taking so much of their time. He said: "Do you eat lunch?" When I said I did, he invited me to go with him. He would pay for the lunch if I would keep on talking. He took me back to the office and invited others in and made me repeat a whole lot of these things that I thought they did not want to hear. I was kept busy until closing time that afternoon. That was my first encounter with the WCC.

In 1952 I was invited to come to the International Missionary Council, extended Assembly, at Willingen, Germany. This was my first experience as a Pentecostal in an ecumenical convention. I checked in for three days, thinking I could not live on cold shoulder for more than that. But when I arrived on the conference floor during coffee-break, Dr. John A. Mackay, who was president of the I.M.C., took me by my arm and went down the line introducing me as his great Pentecostal friend. There was no mistake. I was not evangelical or fundamental, but distinctly *Pentecostal*.

The next day a speaker complained that Christianity had become so institutionalized that it would be a blessing if some of these institutions burned down. Dr. Mackay then informed them that while they were worrying about their institutions, he would like to call on a friend who came from a movement that had encircled the world with missions in less than a half century, and that without institutions. He said to me: "Come and tell us in two five-minute periods *why* and *how* the Pentecostals accomplished so much in so short a time."

I assured the gathering that I did not come to boast about any achievements of the Pentecostals, but in answer to the questions I could only say: "The reason why Pentecostals have been so successful in missions is because they are Pentecostal." Then I noticed a few frowns and I continued: "Gentleman, I did not say it is because we speak with tongues, for if that was all we had from the experience of the baptism in the Holy Spirit, we would have been a forgotten issue long ago. However, Jesus said

'Ye shall receive power,' and that is the secret of our success. Untrained and sometimes illiterate people went forth without boards or institutions to help them, simply guided by the Holy Spirit who confirmed their preaching with 'signs following.' They established beachheads for Christianity in the most unlikely and difficult places, where others had even failed.

"Now for the question: How did you do it? I would say: In the old-fashioned apostolic way of witnessing—each-one-tell-one. It was when the church in Jerusalem was scattered abroad (all except the Apostles) that they went everywhere preaching the Word. Today we scatter the apostles, and the church members have nothing to say. The Pentecostal Movement started out as a witnessing community. However you cannot teach people to be witnesses; they become witnesses when they have an experience of something. The courts of our day will not accept a 'prompted' witness. A good Pentecostal witness is one who can tell how he got saved and healed and baptized in the Holy Spirit. Such a testimony is more powerful than a sermon on salvation and healing and the Holy Spirit."

I stayed at Willingen for the full period of eleven days. I had interviews, by their request, with 110 of the 210 delegates. This then placed me in touch with many of the ecumenical leaders and officers of the World Council of Churches.

In 1954 I was invited by Dr. Visser 't Hooft, the WCC secretary, to go to the Second Assembly at Evanston. When I asked him what he wanted me to do, he told me that I should do exactly what I did at Willingen—just witness and talk to as many as possible about my Pentecostal experiences. When I suggested that I might be mistaken for a "schismatic," trying to cause division among brethren, he assured me that he had been convinced that I had no such intentions, for he had not found anyone in my contacts to whom I had suggested that they should leave their church. I agreed to go, and it was arranged that I could serve on the Staff, the press section. This gave me just the opportunities I needed to talk to archbishops, bishops, professors, and principals and presidents of institutions. Sometimes I kept going until after midnight.

I thought this would be the end of my ecumenical outreach. But in 1956 I was invited to a retreat in Connecticut to speak to a group of ecumenical leaders on the American front. That was one of my greatest experiences in this ministry.

Twenty-four ecumenical leaders were comfortably seated around me. They had invited me to bring them the truth about the Pentecostal experience and the Pentecostal Movement. I was asked to be devastatingly frank. This very request caused me to seek the face of the Lord to be sure that I would meet these friends just as Jesus would have done if He had been there in person. I could remember days when I had wished I could have set my eyes upon such men to denounce their theology and pray the judgment of God upon them for what I considered their heresies and false doctrines. Here was such an opportunity and they said, "Be devastatingly frank." I prayed, "Lord, what would *You* have me to do."

That morning something happened to me. After a few introductory words I suddenly felt a warm glow come over me. I knew this was the Holy Spirit taking over, but what was He doing to me? Instead of the old harsh spirit of criticism and condemnation in my heart, I now felt such love and compassion for these ecclesiastical leaders that I would rather have died for them than pass sentence upon them. All at once I knew that the Holy Spirit was in control and I was beside myself and yet sober as a judge (II Cor. 5:13). Thank God, from that day on I knew what it meant to minister along the "more excellent way" (I Cor. 12:31). This indeed is the technique of the Holy Spirit.

For seventy-five minutes I poured from my heart all that the Spirit gave me. Never have I known a more attentive audience. If things were happening to me, I realized the same Spirit was doing things to my listeners. This was very evident when the time came for questions and answers. There was an unaffected desire to know all about the gifts and ministries of the Holy Spirit. The promise of Jesus was made so real to me: "But when they shall lead you...take no thought beforehand what ye shall speak, neither do ye premeditate: but whatsover shall be given you in that hour, that speak ye: for it is not ye that speak, *but the Holy Ghost*" (Mark 13:11).

Then there came a question that presented an opportunity to be devastatingly frank, but I had no desire to belittle or criticize or hurt anyone. Silently I prayed. The question was: "Please tell us what is the difference between you and us. We quote the same Scriptures as you do, and yet when you say those words they sound so different. We say the same things that you do, but there seems to be a deeper implication in what you say. You have said nothing with which we want to differ and yet there seems to be a distinct difference somewhere." What was I to say? What was the truth? The Spirit came to my rescue, and I said: "Gentlemen, comparisons are odious, and I do not wish to injure anyone's feelings or hurt your pride. But the truth as I see it is this: You have the truth *on ice*, and I have it *on fire*."

"That is too deep for me; please explain," said one.

"Gentlemen, we have been dealing with the meat of the Word," I answered, "so please allow me to illustrate what I mean. I live in Dallas, Texas, where it can become very hot. We have a deep-freeze to preserve food in bulk. When meat is at a reasonable price-level we buy half a steer. Thus I know there is the very best grade of Texas-steer T-bone steak in that freezer. If any of you were to visit my home, I would like to serve you such a steak. Suppose I take it out of the freezer and place it on a plate before you; could you eat it? Of course not. It is just a frozen chunk of iced meat. But we could discuss it. We could even record the facts. It weighs about twelve ounces. It contains so many calories. There are several vitamins in it. We know the butcher who sold it. We may know the ranch that raised the steer. We may know the pedigree of the steer and its age, and so forth. Then we could go the other way and decide, if you eat it, it will satisfy your hunger. It will add to your weight, and so forth. But after half an hour of good "beef discussion," it is still there and we are still hungry. Our minds have been fed with information but the beef was not enjoyed.

"Now what shall we do? Something needs to be done to that meat to make it edible, and make our facts real. I give it to my wife. Without inquiring about our collected facts and information about the steak, she places it on *fire*. Within a few minutes the atmosphere in the house changes and everyone knows something is cooking. My little boy comes in and shouts: 'Mom, something smells good and I am starving.' We are all served a nice hot steak off the fire, and we say, 'That just hits the spot.' Is my little boy going to get sick because he does not know all the facts about the beef?

"You know, gentlemen," I continued, "here we have the elements of a good Pentecostal meeting. There is an atmosphere. Everyone knows something is happening. The old alcoholic that sits there does not have to listen to the theology of saving grace; he is not told the theology or the doctrine of regeneration. He gets the 'hot gospel' stated in facts—God loves you. God will save you. Ask and it shall be given you. Seek and you will find. Do it now. Jesus is here to meet you. He will give you the water of life and you will never thirst again—and the sinner accepts the invitation. In a few minutes he rises from his knees and *knows* something has happened to him. In his life something has hit the spot. He is now a changed man. There will be plenty of time to teach him the doctrine and theology of his experience later on. After all, I submit there was a Pentecostal experience of the baptism in the Holy Ghost in the lives of the Apostles before they ever developed or framed the doctrine and the theology. They had experience and no doctrine. Today most people have doctrine and no experience.

"My friends," I said, "if you will take the great truths of the Gospel out of your theological deep freezers and get them on the fire of the Holy Spirit, your churches will yet turn the world upside down. The Church does not need better theologians but rather men full of faith and of the Holy Ghost (Acts 6:5) —men that will say: 'Our sufficiency is of God; who also hath made us able ministers of the new testament; not of the letter, but of the spirit: for the letter killeth, but the spirit giveth life' (II Cor. 3:5, 6)."

After this, one of those dear men said: "Why did I not meet someone like you many years ago? I realized my ministry was not a success, but I could not find the reason for my failure. Now I discover my spiritual temperature was not right. I lacked the power of the Holy Spirit."

"The Scripture is a key to itself. Besides, we have the Holy Spirit to open it to us.... God is His own interpreter. We fail to understand the Scriptures because we seldom accept His help. This, I feel assured, is the reason why we are so often in ignorance. It is not that the truth sought for is not in the Word, but that

hrough lack of communion with Him who gave the Word, we
ave not enough of His mind to apprehend His meaning, even
vhere He has fully expressed it."—Andrew Jukes in *The Law of
he Offerings*.

My next thrilling experience was the 18th Council of the
'resbyterian World Alliance in Sao Paulo, Brazil, during 1959.
attended as a Pentecostal Fraternal delegate with some 600
ther delegates from 56 countries representing 46 million Calvin-
sts. When the President of the Council, Dr. John A. Mackay, in-
roduced me he remarked: "Whatever else history may have to
ay about our friend, this fact will surely be recorded. This is
he first confessional body that has extended recognition to the
'entecostal Movement as a sound Christian body. The records
vill also show that Princeton Seminary was the first institution
o recognize this by inviting our friend as missions lecturer."

In my heart I thought: How wonderful. Calvinist churches
vere the first to disfellowship members with a Pentecostal ex-
erience at the turn of the century. Now fifty years later, they
ecognize this as the work of the Holy Spirit. I find this is what
s happening all over the world. The climate in the churches is
hanging rapidly.

During the last three years I have had the privilege of lec-
uring at many institutions besides Princeton Seminary. I have
een to Yale Divinity, Union Theological Seminary in New York,
outhern Methodist University in Dallas, Colgates Rochester
chool of Divinity, Fuller's Seminary in Pasadena, British Columbia
Jniversity in Vancouver, the Ecumenical Institutes in Switzerland
nd America, and other centers. After this visit to England and
Iolland I went to the Second Latin American Evangelical Con-
erence in Lima, Peru, in August.

In the past I have not given much publicity to these activ-
ies because I fear that publicity often kills good things. Besides,
did not want to embarrass my friends who were so kind to me,
nd I certainly did not want to exploit my privileges to any per-
onal advantage. Recently a group of Episcopal ministers in
America asked me who sponsored me in this work and what my
osition was now in the Pentecostal Movement. I had to explain
hat this was a faith venture. No one hired me and no one can
re me. I have resigned from every position I held, and so I have

become just a great "has been" insofar as positions are concerned I am a good will ambassador for Christ. I travel as the Lord provides through His people, and He takes care of my family too.

Now in conclusion, let me say what a great honor and privilege it was to be one of the speakers at the recent meeting of the Commission of Faith and Order at St. Andrews, Scotland. There I made contact with some of the Roman Catholic observers. So I have actually had an opportunity to learn all about the Ecumenical Movement, which is greater than the World Council of Churches or the Roman Catholic Church and all the orthodox churches together. From Pentecostalism to Catholicism there are "winds of change" blowing. I pray that these may become again the "mighty rushing wind" of the day of Pentecost.

THE REMARKABLE MOVE OF GOD
IN THE
DENOMINATIONAL CHURCH WORLD

Some travel statistics: June 26 to August 12, 1960

I spent seven weeks visiting eight countries: England, France, Switzerland, Holland, Denmark, Finland, Sweden, and Norway, preaching in twenty-one cities, delivering twenty-one sermons, attending two most important Ecumenical Conferences, participating in thirty conference meetings, meeting with nearly two hundred theologians, having interviews with about one hundred of them, at the same time meeting and having fellowship with eighty-six Pentecostal pastors and leaders. I traveled by air in DC7C, Viscounts, Caravelle and Comet Jets, and by train and car, for a distance of approximately 12,500 miles. I met with archbishops, professors, university presidents, seminary principals, pastors and priests from Latin American lands, African territories, Middle East countries, India, Asia, Japan, Canada, and the United States; from many Western European countries and from lands behind the Iron Curtain. These men belong to the major Protestant confessions. On their registration cards one could see several brands of Lutherans, Episcopalians, Methodists, Baptists, Congregational, Reformed, and Presbyterian churches, and then there were the orthodox churches who are members of the World Council of Churches, and a few orthodox church observers from behind the Iron Curtain. There were also a few observers from the Roman Catholic churches in France and England. I was the only one with Pentecostal Movement on my badge, but thank the Lord, there were others with the Pentecostal experience.

The Reason for This Trip

First, I was invited by the Study Division of the World Coun
cil of Churches to attend a Consultation on Evangelism at the
Ecumenical Institute near Geneva, Switzerland, July 5 to 11. Then
I received an invitation from the World Council to speak to the
Commission on Faith and Order at their gathering August 2 to
10, in St. Andrews University, Scotland. In both of these gather
ings, one of the main topics for discussion was the Holy Spirit

The Consultation on Evangelism

At Chateau de Bossey most of the members of the Consulta
tion had already checked in. Quite a few were old friends whom
I had met at some previous ecumenical conferences over the pas
eight years. Others were renowned churchmen of whom I ha
heard. In welcoming me, most said they were so happy to have
the Pentecostal Movement or revival represented. Some simple
said: "We are so happy to know the Holy Spirit will be repre
sented by one who really knows Him." Sometimes I felt that
was welcomed just like Peter was in the house of Cornelius, b
those who *want* to know the works of God. There were sixty me
from many countries and even more denominations. Evangelis
Billy Graham flew direct from Rio de Janeiro in Brazil where h
had just addressed about 200,000 people in the great wind-up rall
of the Baptist World Alliance meetings. It was so good to talk t
Billy and his associates and to hear his message. His humilit
and evident love simply disarmed his strongest critics.

The opening address on Wednesday morning by Dr. D. T
Niles of Ceylon gave a strong foundation for all discussions an
gave me the strongest encouragement to emphasize the impor
tance of the Holy Spirit in any and all attempts at evangelism b
every member, and every church, and by any preacher or evar
gelist. Dr. Niles pointed out that in many respects Christianit
offered no more than other religions but there were three differ
entia that should always be preached and emphasized. These are
1. To be a real Christian, every man and woman shoul
   have a very definite encounter with the resurrected, livin
   Christ. Simply to accept His teaching intellectually is ne

enough. Other religions have no such vital encounter with the living God.

2. To be a real witness and to minister in New Testament apostolic fashion, every Christian should have a very clear yes or no to the question of St. Paul to the Ephesians in Acts 19.

3. To be ready for His coming, every Christian should live prepared and expecting the coming of the Lord. Other religions have no such hope and expectation. Are we prepared to meet our soon-coming Lord?

Each time when it seemed as if the meeting would move toward a discussion on the teaching of the Lord rather than on Christ himself as the way, the truth and the life, Dr. Markus Barth (son of Professor Karl Barth of Basel) would call them back to the person of Christ. God gave us His Son, not His creed or doctrines which are useless unless we learn to know the living Christ. Then I could add: But only the Holy Spirit can reveal and declare the living Christ, and that is why so much preaching today is sterile and without power. They speak as the Pharisees and not as Christ, with authority. Then I could point out that the Holy Spirit can dwell only in blood-cleansed and redeemed men who have become His temples. Without regeneration there can be no real receiving of the Holy Spirit, and there are two definite experiences. "God has no grandsons"; therefore we cannot inherit these blessings from our forebears but must be born of God to become the sons of God. In the final report, the statement "God has no grandsons" was taken up as fundamental to the reasons for cold and formal Christianity. The whole Consultation was one of the most spiritual and most vital discussions I have ever attended in ecumenical meetings.

The Commission on Faith and Order

On the train from Edinburgh I met with the first group on their way to St. Andrews. We were met by a bus and soon were settled in comfortable rooms in the University Halls. Wednesday morning I quickly hired a typewriter and started writing letters. That morning the meetings began with an introduction of everyone present. I felt a little fearful. Such great renowned men. Such learned professors. What shall I do? But these men were so humble and kind and asked so many questions with such keen interest that I never had any fear again. It was a real encouragement to see Dr. John A. Mackay of Princeton and to be introduced by him to many new friends. I enjoyed every meeting. It seemed as if everyone was talking about the Holy Spirit. Reports and literature were full of the subject, and even the Pentecostal Movement was one of the most frequently mentioned groups. I had to believe that there was more than a passing interest in the Pentecostal revival and a very deep and keen desire to see the Holy Spirit move in the churches again. I greatly enjoyed a short visit from Brother Donald Gee, who attended the meetings during Friday as a visitor.

The Message I Delivered

Friday evening, August 5, the program showed it was my opportunity to be a special speaker and to give my message. I had then seen from others that if they spoke briefly they had more time for questions and answers, so I cut my talk down to fifteen minutes and then had thirty minutes to answer questions. This gave me an opportunity to say what I could not say at first without appearing arrogant and proud. I assured them they could not insult me, for I refuse to take offence from my friends. The questions were sincere and to the point. As usual there came the question: "Do your people still teach that tongues is essential to the baptism of the Holy Spirit?" And as usual I replied, "No, unfortunately not, and where this standard is dropped, there the fervency and power of the revival tends to diminish greatly. It seems that we must either accept all the manifestations of the Spirit in Scriptural order or we lose the power that follows the baptism in the Spirit." (For full text of message see page 29.)

From that meeting onwards, I had the most interesting conversations with many of the leading men in this gathering. On Monday morning, August 8, I had another opportunity to speak in connection with the witnessing of members. How can anyone witness when he has no knowledge or experience of the matter? One must be born again. In this, Dr. Mackay and others backed me strongly. Oh, the battle between the laity and the ministry! It seems that we in the Pentecostal Movement are seeking to develop a stronger ministry and the churches are seeking to get back to a more effective witnessing of the laity. We had that and that is why the Movement has swept the world in less than half a century. Brethren, in the name of Christ I plead, let us not lose the best we ever had—the witness of all members who are filled with the Spirit. Or have we now only tongues? Have we lost the power?

What Next?

As a result of these two international, interdenominational, truly ecumenical gatherings and the Pentecostal testimony I have been able to bring to this level of the ecclesiastical world, many more doors are opening for ministry in seminaries and other institutions. When I say that I cannot possibly keep up with it all, they say: "But can you not find others among your brethren with a burden for this kind of ministry? Please find us more men full of fire and love like yourself." The harvest is ripe, but the laborers are very few.

When I now see the results of this ministry which I began in 1952 and the tremendous changes that the Holy Spirit has brought about in the great World Council of Churches, then I feel that I want to keep going from one seminary and one conference to another. There are now hundreds of hearts that have been getting prepared for a real Pentecostal outpouring. Hundreds that were violently opposed to any such idea are now asking, "What must we do when it comes?" This is a great field with tremendous possibilities. When I say that I feel the Pentecostal revival inside the churches may yet become the greater of the two—one outside, the other inside—I really mean it. When these dry bones have come "bone to his bone" and the sinews of the Word begin to grip them, and when the flesh of God's grace begins to cover them, it will be a great and a mighty army for God. They have all the equipment and only lack the power of the Spirit to set in motion a movement that will indeed turn the world upside down.

I rejoice in great mass meetings and in mass movements, but I feel much happier in this ministry of reaching the shepherds and the leaders rather than their flocks, for if the shepherds turn to the Lord, they will soon bring the sheep back to the true shepherd—Christ. He will again baptize them with the Holy Spirit and with fire.

A Few Conclusions

These meetings and many other personal contacts have convinced me that during the last decade, an entirely new spiritual climate has come into the great historic churches of Protestantism. My conclusion does not stem from spasmodic upsurges that we find here and there. I can discern a deep spiritual stir in the hearts of all ranks, but particularly do I find a sincere recognition of the work of the Holy Spirit among the top echelons of Protestantism. The opposition to and the criticism of mysterious and supernatural manifestations of the Spirit has been replaced by more than a casual interest in a true revival of the charismata in the church. Divine healing is now almost universally accepted and is commonly practiced by most confessions. The baptism in the Holy Spirit is no longer mentioned in evasive terms and with hushed undertones. Even speaking in other tongues is receiving more and more favorable attention and is being recognized as a manifestation of the Spirit for our time.

THE ECUMENICAL MOVEMENT

There are many today who make a study of the Ecumenical Movement to find what is wrong with it. Diligently they seek out men and statements that appear liberal and socialistic, and then seek to blanket the whole Movement with the few "exceptions" that they have discovered. On this basis I have every reason to blanket the Ecumenical Movement with a "conclusion" that they are Pentecostal. Not only does their published literature propagate strong Pentecostal teachings, but there are now many Spirit-filled, yes indeed, "tongues-speaking" ministers in the National and World Council of Churches. I shall not be surprised when our fundamentalist friends who attack the Pentecostals as severely as they do the World Council, begin to "expose" the Pentecostal trend within the ranks of the Ecumenical Movement.

The Holy Spirit has never recognized barriers. He goes to the synagogue as well as to the heathen temple. He moves upon Jews, Samaritans, and Gentiles. He goes to "Jerusalem," to "all Judea," to "Samaria," and "to the uttermost parts." He is universal in His operations and ecumenical in His outreach. The prophet of God said the Holy Spirit would come upon all flesh. He moves upon the *oikoumene*—all humanity. Sectarianism militates directly against the work of the Holy Spirit. Jesus did not say He would come to organize churches but that He would empower believers to witness in all the world.

During the first few months of 1960, I had wonderful fellowship on the East Coast and the West Coast as well as in the Midwest states. In a non-denominational retreat in New York City, a well-known fundamentalist friend said to me: "I regret to have to admit the fact that my fundamentalist associates almost everywhere are today the most adamant enemies of the Pentecostal

27

Movement." In further discussions my friend also admitted that they recognized that the Pentecostals are thoroughly fundamental in their acceptance of the Scriptures, whilst they are extremely liberal in their spiritual experiences.

Indeed we not only believe the truth, but we appropriate the promises of God and find by experience that Jesus Christ is the same yesterday and today and forever. He saves and sanctifies and baptizes in the Holy Spirit. He heals the sick just as He did in His ministry in the flesh and continued to do in His ministry by the Holy Spirit in His followers and believers from the day of Pentecost. The New Testament is not a record of what happened in one generation, but it is a blueprint of what should happen in every generation until Jesus comes. Every generation must be regenerated by the Spirit. Every regenerated generation must receive the Holy Spirit. Every Spirit-filled generation must live and preach and do the works of God just like Jesus did and just like the Apostles did and like those who followed after the Apostles. It was by the Spirit that Jesus ministered. It was by the Spirit that the Apostles ministered and did the works that Jesus did. By the Spirit we must now expect "greater works than these" in our day.

A Change of Spiritual Climate

From 1900 to 1908 the historic Protestant churches fought the Pentecostal revival and denounced it as of the devil. From 1950 to 1958, the climate has changed and their attitude reversed. During these years I had only occasional contacts and noticed the great change. In 1961 I beheld the results of the change and can declare the Pentecostal revival within the churches is gathering force and speed. The most remarkable thing is that this revival is found in the so-called liberal societies and much less in the evangelical and not at all in the fundamentalist segments of Protestantism. The last-mentioned are now the most vehement opponents of this glorious revival because it is in the Pentecostal Movement and in the modernist World Council Movements that we find the most powerful manifestations of the Spirit. This seems to be true almost without exception in most parts of the world, as far as I know.

DEVELOPMENTS WITHIN THE ECUMENICAL SCENE

The Worldwide Pentecostal Movement

A paper read by David J. du Plessis on August 5, 1960, at St. Andrews, Scotland, before the Commission on Faith and Order of the World Council of Churches.

Kindly allow me a word of personal testimony. I was born in South Africa and at the age of twelve, through the ministry of Spirit-filled Africans, I came to conversion and was born again. In 1918 I received the Holy Spirit as the disciples did on the day of Pentecost. Immediately I began to witness to the saving and sanctifying power of Christ. Soon I was recognized as a young lay preacher. In 1928 I was ordained to full-time ministry. From 1935 I served as Secretary General of the Apostolic Faith Mission of South Africa until I was called to be Secretary of the World Conference of Pentecostal Churches in 1948, and I moved my family to the United States.

Early in 1951 I met with Dr. John Mackay in Princeton, New Jersey, and under his guidance became interested in the Ecumenical Movement, and attended the International Missionary Council in Willingen in 1952. At this time I met Dr. Visser t' Hooft and became acquainted with many leading executives and theologians in the World Council and International Missionary Council. Indeed, it has been a pleasure and a great privilege to keep in close contact with all ecumenical movements in the world during the last decade. I have witnessed and experienced the most astonishing developments.

My Pentecostal brethren and I were somewhat surprised in 1954 when we learned, through Bishop Lesslie Newbegin's book

The Household of God, that at last we were recognized in what we have always considered our true perspective—that is, not a schismatic Protestant group, but rather a fresh revival of New Testament apostolic witness and Pentecostal power. We were not quite so pleased when in 1955 Dr. Henry van Dusen described us as a new reformation. Pentecostalists are staunch believers in regeneration and view a mere reformation with deep suspicion. I think Dr. van Dusen was forgiven in 1958 when in *Life* Magazine he wrote: "Many features of this 'new Christianity' bear striking resemblance to the life of the earliest Christian churches as revealed in the New Testament.... Peter and Barnabas and Paul might find themselves more at home in a Holiness service or at a Pentecostal revival than in the formalized and sophisticated worship of other churches, Catholic or Protestant." In fact he was quoted by most American speakers at the Fifth Pentecostal World Conference in Toronto in August 1958. *Life* Magazine described it as the "fastest-growing Christian movement in the world today, one so dynamic that it stands with Catholicism and historic Protestantism as a third force in Christendom."

At the turn of this century there was no Pentecostal Movement. Today it consists of a community of more than ten million souls that can be found in almost every country under the sun. About ten percent of non-Catholic missionaries on the field are Pentecostal. That is about 3,500. In Italy and some other countries the Pentecostal membership exceeds that of all other non-Catholic churches. This was not brought about by a planned strategy from some central point. In fact, up to 1947 there were large movements in many corners of the earth that knew nothing of one another. In a sense, in many countries it is the most indigenous Christian movement of this age. In fact, in the beginning of the century, just the news of what was happening in one city would set aflame the hearts in another city and a new revival would result from simple cottage prayer meetings.

The firmness with which the historic churches rejected this Pentecostal experience caused their members, who came to enjoy this blessing, to leave the church and begin new assemblies. After ten years so many new and independent local assemblies had been established that it was felt there should be some kind of fellowship to safeguard sound doctrine and to correct the many forms of fanaticism that were threatening to wreck the whole revival. Thus from 1910 onwards, there developed a number of Fellowships in many areas and countries of the world. The nature and form of organization that was adopted by them varied according to the influence of the historic churches upon the new Pentecostal leaders. It is now clear that most of them followed the system of autonomous local churches linked by Regional and National Fellowship Conventions. All kinds of names were adopted. The most popular of these is The Assemblies of God, also translated into French, Italian, Spanish, Portuguese, and other languages. Then there followed the Church of God with a number of prefixes and suffixes, such as, Pentecostal Church of God, and Church of God in Christ. Besides these there are Apostolic Faith churches and missions, Pentecostal Holiness Church, Open Bible Standard churches, International Foursquare and Elim Foursquare churches, and a variety of others.

Since the first World Conference of 1947, the Pentecostal Ecumenical Movement has developed to where about 90 percent of the entire revival around the world is now represented at the Triennial World Conference. At the world level, there is an amazing unity in spirit, but at the local level cooperation and even recognition of one another is still sadly lacking. "But why worry" said a friend of mine. "We are all growing in membership and the revival is still on." Pentecostals are more concerned about maintaining spiritual life and missionary zeal than in developing unity. If Paul and Barnabas cannot agree, then let us have two revival teams instead of one. Their implicit faith in the work of the Holy Spirit in the lives of men and in the Spirit-filled community causes Pentecostals to leave many of their problems to be solved by the Spirit in His own time. There is a strong desire always to be able to say: "It seemed good to the Holy Spirit and to us." It is generally accepted that only by the Holy Spirit are we all baptized into one body and only He knows who truly belong to the body, the Church Universal. Whatever man may do, the Holy Spirit will ultimately bring about the unity and its manifestation. All we should do is to keep filled with the Spirit and humbly follow His guidance. It is this very principle that brings me to these gatherings.

During the last ten years the climate in the historic churches with regard to the Pentecostal movements has changed considerably. There has developed within the ecumenical scene a very keen and sincere interest in the phenomena of the Holy Spirit. Contrary to the expectation and perhaps wishful thinking of church leaders and theologians of fifty years ago, the Pentecostal revival did not blow over to be forgotten, but rather it is blowing all over the world and continues to challenge the churches. Often the question is asked, "What is at the root of the success of the Pentecostal revival? What was it that made them flourish when the entire ecclesiastical world was against them?"

There is only one answer. Christ said: "Ye shall receive *power*, after that the Holy Ghost is come upon you: and ye shall be witnesses unto me" (Acts 1:8). The greatest phenomena has never been the speaking in other tongues but rather the power of the Spirit and the resultant effective witnessing. We are great believers in the priesthood of all believers, and we have been far more interested in apostolic power than in apostolic succession.

Since the Apostles enjoyed a Pentecostal experience before there ever developed a Pentecostal doctrine or theology, we believe that no one can ever grasp the full meaning of the charismata until there is an experience similar to that on the day of Pentecost. If in Samaria they could receive the Holy Spirit after Pentecost, and if ten years after Pentecost the first Gentiles in the house of Cornelius could enjoy this blessing so that Peter could report to the brethren in Jerusalem: "The Holy Ghost fell on them, *as on us*, at the beginning" (Acts 11:15), and if twenty years after Pentecost, Paul could ask the Ephesian believers "Have ye received the Holy Ghost since ye believed?" then surely there was no thought that this experience should fade out of the church. We dare to believe that the blessing is as valid 2,000 years after Pentecost as it was twenty years after the first outpouring of the Spirit. We not only dare to believe, but we dare to receive. That makes all the difference.

The churches ignored the Pentecostal blessing as an existential reality so long that the Pentecostal movements began to feel it was their exclusive inheritance and that the rest of the Christian world would never come back to it. Many of them began to visualize the possibility of the Movement becoming the Church of Christ in the closing days of time. However, this situation has completely changed during the last ten years. Many of my brethren are now convinced that the Lord Jesus Christ, the head of the Church, will pour out His Spirit upon all flesh and that the historic churches will be revived or renewed and then in this renewal be united by the Holy Spirit himself.

Not only have the many Pentecostal societies become united in national and international fellowships in the last decade, but they have also accepted the hand of fellowship from the so-called evangelical defections from the mainstreams of Protestantism. This association with evangelicals has, however, caused them to be violently opposed to the World Council of Churches. But at this very point there is now a new development on the ecumenical scene.

The World Evangelical Fellowship can claim to have large Pentecostal societies in their ranks, and the World Council has none. On the other hand, there now are large numbers of ministers within the National Councils and the World Council that are enjoying the same glorious Pentecostal experience that the Pentecostals have, and yet they are still loyal to their own confessions and have not been disfellowshipped by their brethren. I personally know many Lutheran, Reformed, Episcopalian, Methodist and Baptist ministers who are "filled with the Holy Spirit...speaking in other tongues as the Spirit [gives] them utterance." Actually, I am privileged to share in two Pentecostal revivals: one still outside the World Council of Churches, and the other more recent one, inside the historic churches within the Ecumenical Movement. I can see that the revival or renewal within the churches may yet become the greatest and most powerful of the two.

When John the Baptist addressed the religious leaders of his day in preparation for the revelation of their Messiah, he left them only one awful choice when he said: "Now also the ax is laid unto the root of the trees: therefore every tree which bringeth not forth good fruit is hewn down, and cast into the fire." This is holocaust. Then he continued: "I indeed baptize you with water unto repentance: but he that cometh after me is mightier than I...he shall baptize you with the Holy Ghost, and with fire." That is Pentecost. Is not the prophetic message of the Spirit who is preparing the Church or the Parousia much the same in our time? Has the Church any other choice? I believe it is Pentecost or holocaust—enduement or judgment.

I agree with Dr. Ernest Wright of Harvard when he writes in his recent book *The Rule of God*, "God, through the work of the Spirit, has always been at war with human institutionalism, because the institution becomes idolatrous, self-perpetuating, and self-worshipping, because church membership becomes synonymous with the new birth, because man tries to make the Spirit follow law.

"Christian history has shown that the charisma has a way of breaking out of all bounds, of achieving the unexpected, and of violating institutional proprieties."

I particularly endorse this statement: "It is important to observe that in prophetic eschatology the consummation of the kingdom of God is to be marked by a great revival of charismatic happenings. Both leaders and people will then be Spirit-filled and Spirit-empowered on a scale hitherto unknown." My prayer and hope is that this will soon be seen everywhere in the world, so that the Church can once again "turn the world upside down."

In conclusion, I want to say with Dr. Henry van Dusen: "The call to the ministry is to be alert to discern every movement of the living, confounding, uncontrollable Spirit of God in what someone has called 'His sovereign unpredictability.' " May God bless the Commission on Faith and Order and make them a blessing.

MISSIONS LECTURES

During May 1959 I spent three weeks on the campus of Princeton Seminary as the guest of the president, Dr. John A. Mackay. It was at this time that I was invited to return later in the year as missions lecturer.

When I arrived this second time, Dr. Mackay had retired and the new president, Dr. James McCord, welcomed me. I am deeply grateful to him and the faculty for their kindness and encouragement during my stay. I cherish many sacred memories of my visits to Princeton Seminary.

Missions Lecture I

THE HOLY SPIRIT IN THE LIFE OF THE INDIVIDUAL

You have already learned from the introduction by Dr. McCord that I have a Pentecostal background of some importance, and I am sure you would expect me to speak with deep spiritual convictions as well as from a wide experience in the work of the Holy Spirit.

I am happy to witness to the fact that I have known this life in the power of the Spirit for many years. I thank God for the first great change in my life that I experienced in 1916 when I met Christ as my Saviour. This came about through the life and testimony of black African Christians. You may think this is "mission in reverse"—a little white heathen converted through the ministry of black Christians. It was the undeniable manifestation of the Holy Spirit in their lives that brought me to realize that I was a sinner who needed a Saviour. Thank the Lord, He found me and saved me.

After my conversion I began to study the Bible and soon discovered that Jesus is not only the Lamb of God who will take away sin, but He is also the one who is to baptize with the Holy Spirit and with fire. The change in my life by the work of the Holy Spirit had made me a temple of the Spirit of God, so I began to seek this baptism in the Spirit. In 1918, Christ, the mighty Baptizer, met me and overwhelmed me with the fullness of the Holy Spirit. I have enjoyed a life of rich spiritual adventure for more than forty years.

Now that you have heard the testimony of this individual, let us proceed to deal with the life of any or every individual. We must always deal with the person. This is where missionary vision begins. In these days of mass movements we are forgetting that God deals with the individual. Only Christianity emphasizes the great value of the individual. "God is no respecter of persons: but in every nation he [the individual] that feareth him...is accepted with him" (Acts 10:34, 35). Preach the Gospel to every creature. Go and find your first convert to Christ.

In the Old Testament God promised a new covenant through the prophet Ezekiel. In chapter 36 verse 26 we read: "A new heart also will I give you, and a new spirit will I put within you." This indicates a real change of heart and of spirit—indeed an actual change of character and temperament. But in the 27th verse God says: "And I will put *my spirit* within you." This is more than a "new spirit." This has been emphasized by Pentecostals for the last fifty years, and it has caused some controversies with the historic churches. We believe that when you accept the redemptive work of Calvary, you are changed by the Holy Spirit and you receive a "new spirit." But there is more to follow. We believe that when God says "I will put my spirit within you," it has reference to the baptism in the Holy Spirit.

When we come to the New Testament, we find John the Baptist looking beyond the crowd, and pointing to Jesus he says: "Behold the Lamb of God, which taketh away the sin of the world." This implies a great change, for sin is man's great problem. Here is a challenge to accept redemption from sin and become a child of God, from whom sin has separated us. However, John then said something more: "He shall baptize you with the Holy

Ghost." This is more than taking away sin and changing a man's heart. This baptism means: "I will put *my spirit* within you."

Let me remind you of the message of John to the religious leaders of his generation. According to Matthew he said, "Every tree which bringeth not forth good fruit is hewn down, and cast into the fire." This is judgment; this is holocaust. "But he that cometh after me...shall baptize you with the Holy Ghost, and with fire." This is enduement. This is Pentecost. Do we have any other choice today? For me it remains: Pentecost at any cost.

Thus far we have checked with the Old Testament and then with the last prophet of the old dispensation, who was the first of the new. Now let us see what Jesus has to say on the subject. "Ye know him, for he dwelleth with you and *shall be in you*." The Holy Spirit was with the disciples because He was in Christ.

Jesus received the Spirit at His baptism in Jordan. When people ask me whether I consider this baptism in the Holy Spirit as absolutely essential in Christian experience, I point them to Jesus. He was born of the Spirit, the very Son of God. This fact might have enabled Him to minister without further enduement. But that was not the case. At the age of thirty He received the Holy Spirit. From that moment on His life changed. He did not return to the carpenter shop.

Now what did the Holy Spirit do in Christ's life? He led Him into the wilderness where He was forty days tempted of the devil. Many become confused when after great spiritual adventures, they discover the enemy is more real than ever. When people tell me they do not know much about the devil and demonism, I must conclude that they do not know the Holy Spirit either. If they were full of the Spirit, they would quickly discern and detect the spirit of evil. Satan would challenge them as he challenged the Lord Jesus Christ. In fact, I make it a point to warn those who seek a life of fullness in the Spirit also to prepare for spiritual battles.

After defeating the enemy with the Word, Jesus returned from the wilderness. In His first sermon in Nazareth He declared: "The Spirit of the Lord is upon me," and He accepted the program of service that the Lord had given Him with this anointing. I consider that when we follow the Master, we may expect the same blessings, the same enduement, and the same program. Jesus said:

"As my Father hath sent me, even so send I you." This is a divine equation: born of the Spirit, then anointed with the Spirit, and empowered for the ministry. Therefore He instructed His disciples "that they should not depart from Jerusalem, but wait for the promise of the Father...ye shall be baptized with the Holy Ghost not many days hence."

In the 16th chapter of St. John, Jesus explained to the disciples that "when he is come, he will reprove the world of sin, and of righteousness, and of judgment." Recently a professor asked me: "How could you tell that the Holy Spirit is working in the life of an individual?" My answer was: "When I see a man is unhappy and getting more uncomfortable when I speak to him, I realize the Holy Spirit is bringing him under conviction. That is why he is disturbed and possibly confused. I never send such a person to a psychiatrist to settle his nerves. I lead him to Christ to settle the sin-question." The professor expected me, as a Pentecostal, to say, "The Spirit is upon him when I hear him speak with tongues." Oh no. The Spirit is first upon him to bring conviction; then after cleansing from sin, the Spirit comes within to manifest himself in speaking with tongues.

Since the day of Pentecost the Holy Spirit has constantly been at work upon the lives of men from generation to generation. Many of the disturbances in the lives of individuals today cannot be explained. But I believe it is the Holy Spirit at work, convincing men of sin and sensitizing the conscience. Here lies the great difference between Christianity and Communism. The Holy Spirit sensitizes the conscience, while satanic forces sear the conscience and by brainwashing try to annihilate it. This sensitizing process often begins when a person who seems to be perfectly satisfied with life comes to church and under the hearing of a powerful sermon becomes greatly disturbed. I have heard people say to their friends who invited them to church: "We shall not go there again because your preacher seemed to know all about us. It was nice of you to invite us to the service, but it was not nice of you to tell the pastor about us."

The Holy Spirit forever remains the guide into all truth. He is busy in this very meeting. I do not have to talk in tongues to prove to you that He is within. He may be speaking a word of knowledge and thus answer your questions. He may speak a word of wisdom and solve your problems. I was deeply impressed by what John Garrett, Director of the Information Office of the WCC in Geneva, wrote recently: "Do we think of the Spirit as *Him*, as God, the judging, purifying maker of our lives, who destroys evil, and therefore cannot tolerate us as we are—self-important, self-satisfied, self-absorbed?... A church that takes Pentecost seriously knows that it must wait for God himself to change it from a church of Pharisees into a church of Christian witnesses." (See page 107.)

The first truth that dawns on a person upon whom the Holy Spirit moves is the fact and the guilt of sin. Then He reveals the resurrected living Christ as Saviour and again as the mighty Baptizer in the Spirit. Christ had no sin, but His life changed when the Holy Spirit came upon Him. The Apostles changed after He came into their lives on the day of Pentecost. I have seen tens of thousands change in my own generation.

Allow me to tell a little of my own experience. I grew up in a very strict and pietistic home. My father was not a missionary but he was a builder. While he was building a home for missionaries, I was able to see what the Holy Spirit could do in the lives of pagans. He made them powerful witnesses to their compatriots. They had something to tell and to demonstrate by their lives, which had changed from the darkness of witchcraft to the light of purity, honesty, and charity. I became desperate in my hunger for this wonderful life in the Spirit. But I noticed that people who enjoyed the power to witness in word and in deed were those who spoke with tongues. I had read of that in the book of Acts, and now I saw it and heard it with my own ears. I knew it was true, it was real.

Earlier in this lecture I mentioned that I received the baptism in the Spirit during 1918. I knew He had come into my life, for I spoke with tongues. Now I realize that tongues would make a subject in itself, but I am merely witnessing to the fact that I know this manifestation of the Spirit. Once a professor asked me: "Why do you always emphasize tongues?" With a smile I asked him: "Sir, why do you always oppose tongues?" You see, anyone will always defend the issue on which he is attacked. Personally I encourage no one to seek for a "tongues experience" but rather for a baptism that is true to the Pentecostal pattern.

By way of simple illustration let us take a man that goes into a shoe store to buy a pair of shoes. He never mentions the tongues in the shoes. He knows they go with the shoes. Why not accept the baptism in the Spirit just like Jesus gave it on the day of Pentecost when they all spake with tongues as the Spirit gave utterance?

Another professor asked me: "Is not tongues considered the least of all the gifts?" I replied: "Sir, I believe it is, and that is why I suggest that everyone begin with this manifestation of the Spirit."

However, Jesus never said, "Ye shall speak with tongues"; rather He emphasized: "Ye shall be witnesses." I must not conclude this talk without stressing this point. People who are baptized in the Spirit and then continue to walk in the Spirit are not primarily "tongue-talkers," but they become inveterate "talkers" or witness for Christ the Saviour.

Witnessing to the power and grace of the Lord Jesus is a very important aspect of the Holy Spirit in the life of the individual. This has been the great secret of the success of the Pentecostal Movement. From my earliest contacts with these people I can remember their extraordinary stress on personal testimony. I was just a boy in those days, but I was encouraged to testify in high school at the time, and I recollect how the principal admonished me not to witness on the school grounds any more because the parents complained that I was disturbing their children.

The outline of my testimony was usually: Jesus is our Saviour, our Healer, the Baptizer in the Holy Spirit, and the soon-coming King. Some have called this the four squares of the Gospel. I must have been convincing on the soon coming of the Lord because it was said the children could not sleep for fear the Lord might come that night.

It seemed as if I could not stop witnessing. If I did not witness on the campus, then I did it on the street, but I had to witness. At the same time I continued to be an A-grade student, so the teachers could not object to my exceptional Christian activities. I heard one of the teachers say: "This boy has something irresistible in him." Yes, that was the Holy Spirit. Some of the very ones that mocked and scoffed at me then are today enjoying the same blessing.

I remember a conversation with the Prime Minister of Southern Rhodesia. I was Executive Secretary of the Pentecostal Movement in South Africa and we were having difficulties in this territory north of us. The Prime Minister said: "The trouble with the people in your church is that they bite off more than they can chew." Remembering that Rhodesia was a tobacco-growing country, I replied, "Sir, we do not chew tobacco." He saw the joke and went on to explain, saying, "Your people preach on the street and convert a drunkard on Saturday night. The next week they baptize him; the following week he receives the Spirit. Then the following week he buds forth as a preacher. In just four weeks they have turned a drunkard into a preacher."

You see, my friend did not know the real difference between a witness and a preacher. But he continued to say that a man would go back to his people, even across the borders in neighboring territories, and would preach there and get converts. This was where all the troubles arose. The man would tell what happened to him. Then he would pray for the people and the same things would happen to them. The next thing, you would find a hut had been turned into a chapel, and a church was born.

I am still dealing with the Spirit in the life of the individual, and here I am speaking of churches being born. But that is exactly how the first-century churches were found in the homes of believers who witnessed. That is how the Pentecostal Movement has spread around the world in less than half a century. It always begins with the individual and with a very personal experience of salvation and the baptism in the Holy Spirit.

The first forty years of my life I spent in Africa. I saw that most of the missionaries tried to make "foreigners" instead of Christians out of Africans. They took great pains to make them Roman Catholics, Lutherans, Calvinists, and Methodists. Actually the worst was when there were some German Lutherans and and other national brands of the same confession. My whole being rebelled against this kind of mission.

Our Pentecostal missions flourished because we did not have books of creeds or catechisms to teach the Africans. We gave them the Bible and told them to believe what is there, and the missionary lived the life that only the Holy Spirit can cause men to live. The Pentecostal Church among the Africans, and for that matter among most nations, becomes an indigenous church with very little effort. The Holy Spirit creates these churches. Tomorrow night we shall deal with the Holy Spirit in the Church.

Missions Lecture II

THE HOLY SPIRIT IN THE LIFE OF THE CHURCH

One day last May after chapel service Dr. Mackay introduced me to Dr. Tom Torrance and Dr. Markus Barth, the son of the great Professor Karl Barth. Dr. Barth looked puzzled. He recognized me because he had heard me preach in Switzerland while he was a student, but he could not remember where we had met before. When I reminded him, he said, "But you were a Pentecostal then. Are you still?" "Oh, yes, worse than ever," I replied. "Then what are you doing here?" he asked. "I am visiting the seminary upon the invitation of Dr. Mackay," I answered. Rather astonished he asked, "Do you mean to tell me Dr. Mackay invited you on this campus to expose these students to the teaching and life of a Pentecostal leader?" I said, "Yes." "Well, that is certainly wonderful," was his rejoinder. "Do you really think so?" I asked. Then he said, "Yes, it will be wonderful if you will do one thing." I felt excited and said: "Please tell me. I need advice." "Well," he said, "do not acquire or employ the high, dry, cold theological terminology that they use in these institutions, but continue to speak the humble, simple, warm creative language of the Holy Spirit that reaches the hearts of men." I said, "Thank you, you are most encouraging. That is the only language I know. But I will not be as foolish as some who quote Saint Paul who said 'I count all things loss for the excellency of Christ' and then they have nothing to lose. I shall minimize the importance of theology or of theological terminology, because I do not possess a great knowledge of it. By the grace of God I shall be just a Pentecostal witness."

Our subject tonight is "The Holy Spirit in the Life of the Church."

Very appropriately Dr. Piper read that famous 12th chapter of Corinthians that deals with this matter. The Apostle wrote this after a ripe experience. I must remind you that before they could write this theology there was an experience. Today we have a great complaint in the world: so much of good theology and doctrine and so little real experience. Men do not have what the Apostles had, and yet their entire theology is based on apostolic writings. I marvel at their knowledge, but I am shocked to find that in spite of all this knowledge, there is still a lack of the personal experience which the early church enjoyed in such abundance.

Dr. S. A. Keen, a Methodist Episcopalian, once wrote: "How presumptuous for us to attempt our mission without the anointing of the Spirit, when Jesus did not venture to enter upon His without the aid of the Spirit. How careful He was to guard His disciples against venturing on their mission without the anointing of the Holy Ghost."

I do not think it will be too much said if we were to declare that when all ministers in all Protestant churches have the same anointing that the Apostles had, the world will be won for Christ in less than a generation. It is the work of the Holy Spirit within the church that counts. We have everything desirable for doing Christian work today except this enduement with the power of the Holy Spirit. Without that, how feeble, comparatively speaking, are our efforts when measured against the great triumphs of the Christians in the first century. Dr. Sam Shoemaker wrote recently: "The churches do not lack for scholars and great minds. They do lack for men and women who can, and will be, channels of the power of God in our day. They lack that which in Pentecost is repeatable and accessible."

Allow me to emphasize here that I do not suggest that any one should leave his church and go to a Pentecostal assembly to get this blessing. That is not necessary. I think I am through forever with the "come-outism" that some people teach. Jesus prayed and said: "I pray not that thou shouldest take them out of the world, but that thou shouldest keep them from evil. They are not of the world, even as I am not of the world" (John 17:15, 16). One who changes his position by coming "out" will never change the world. But one who is changed within by the Spirit is no longer *of* the world even though he is still *in* the world. Changed people will change situations.

Furthermore, the blessing of which I am speaking and to which I can give personal witness was never intended for a society or a denomination. It is a thousand pities that the Pentecostals are being spoken of as a new denomination. Recently in *Life* Magazine, Dr. Henry P. van Dusen wrote of them as the "third force." Some have interpreted this to mean third class, but I do not think that was what the writer had in mind. This should indeed be a force in Christianity and not a competitive denomination.

I consider that the birth or beginning of the Church came about by a spiritual blessing that came into the lives of the Apostles and all their followers. Last night I pointed out how the Holy Spirit worked through the life of Christ. He exhorted His disciples not to leave Jerusalem until they had been endued with the same power that He had. He had promised them that they would do the works that He did and greater works too (John 14:12). Then came the day of Pentecost. They saw tongues of fire. They spoke with unknown tongues, or new tongues as far as they were concerned. I do not agree with the teaching that this happened in order to propagate the Gospel. All who heard them were Jews who came from foreign countries, not foreigners. They heard the languages of the people among whom they lived before they came to Jerusalem for the feast. They could all understand the same language. There is no indication that Peter's sermon was interpreted. This phenomenon of speaking with tongues was a brand new experience that came with this mighty baptism into the Holy Spirit.

Soon the upper-room experience passed away. A few days later two of the Apostles were on their way to the temple. I always emphasize the fact that they went up to pray, not for the purpose of conducting a healing service. On their way they met a challenge—a beggar at the Beautiful Gate. He was asking for charity. Spirit-filled Peter sensed that the Lord wanted to do something different. Boldly he said, "Silver and gold have I none; but such as I have give I thee." A miracle happened. The man was instantly healed, and so perfectly that he could leap with joy.

The Spirit was in action through the Church. A modern newspaper would have carried headlines something like this: *"Jesus Christ Is Back in Town"*—and indeed He was. Not in person, but in His new body—the Church—by the Holy Spirit. He had promised, "I am with you always." Also, "He that dwelleth *with* you shall be *in* you." Now the Apostles knew that He meant what He said. He was with them and He was in them.

On the day of Pentecost 3,000 were added to the Church. On the day of this miracle 5,000 more were added. What phenomenal growth. When the Apostles appeared before the religious authorities of that day, they declared that this was done not in their own power and holiness but in the name of Jesus. They preached Christ, not by repeating His teaching, but by doing the same works that He did. From here on the whole record, according to the Acts of the Apostles, was the work of the Holy Spirit in and through the Church. It could also be called "The Acts of the Holy Spirit."

When we come to Acts 10 we find that a problem arose. They had racial issues in those days. Racialism is nothing new. But the Holy Spirit knows how to break even such barriers. Peter had preached with great power. He had done great miracles. God had used him in a singular way. Yet it is evident from the record that he had not gone to the Gentiles. No one had as yet gone to them, and the Church was almost ten years old. Then Peter was challenged by the Holy Spirit not to call any man common or unclean, and the Spirit bade him go to the house of Cornelius. When he preached Christ to this household, "the Spirit fell on them," the record says, "as at the beginning." So we call this the "Gentile Pentecost." This was another beginning. This was the Church moving into another dimension by the Spirit. This was an extension of the Church into the Gentile world. This was the beginning of missions through the Church.

The Jewish Christians in Jerusalem were not happy about this. They offered all kinds of objections. No revival has ever gone through peacefully. Rather, revivals usually disturb the peace of the world. Jesus said, "My peace I give unto you: not as the world giveth."

Not long ago someone called a group of ministers together without my knowledge, just because he knew I was coming that way. I was asked to talk to them. When I asked them what they wanted me to speak about, they said: "We understand you have a solution to the problems of ministers who feel their ministry is failing." I warned them that "this solution" would solve the problem of powerlessness, but it would create many new problems in the Church.

Peter had to appear before his brethren in Jerusalem to defend his actions. His defense was to place the responsibility on the Holy Spirit. He said, "I was in a trance." Oh how I wish church leaders would fall into such trances today as Peter and Paul did in their day. "I saw a vision," said Peter. Then he explained what it all meant. And as if he knew that the brethren recognized only the Holy Spirit, he declared: *"The Spirit bade me go with them, nothing doubting."* That solved the problem. The Church acknowledged the right of way for the Holy Spirit in their activities. *He* was the Chief Executive, not the Board of Apostles in Jerusalem. In that generation the racial barrier was overcome by the Spirit. But why is it still with us today?

Churches have established traditions. Even during the past fifty years the Pentecostal movements have already established their own traditions in many things. In the beginnings of this movement we tried to follow only what we could learn from the Acts of the Apostles and the Epistles. We recognized the Holy Spirit for teaching and guidance. There was simply one qualification for every member: no one was allowed to teach in Sunday school or hold any office in the church until they were baptized in the Holy Spirit. They were not always cultured and educated people. Often they were poor and illiterate. But right there, for me, is found the miracle of the Holy Spirit in the Church. He can use, and He has used, from the days of ignorant and unlearned fishermen, people with no theological training nor even academic training. He made them His instruments to sweep through a village, town, or city, with such a powerful testimony that multitudes of lives were changed.

The article that I referred to last night, by John Garrett, from the headquarters of the World Council of Churches, asks the question: "Why are the Pentecostal churches thriving? Some people say it is because they specialize in popular music and are not afraid to let their hair down. The worshippers feel at home because they can forget to be respectable and just enjoy themselves. There are many ways of explaining why popular sects grow and thrive all over the world; but no explanation is good enough if it leaves out their stress on the Holy Spirit and the coming of the

Spirit upon the assembled disciples. Such people are dynamic, missionary. A real Christian is identifiable partly by his joy, controlled excitement, and missionary concern. Is it not true that since Pentecost, every Christian is called to be a 'Pentecostalist'?"

I shall never cease to be grateful to the World Council of Churches for letting this "release" go out into the world. It has helped me so much to prove the reason for my zeal in ecumenical ministry when I am being questioned and criticized for my adventures into the realms of the ecumenical movements. Many have thought that there was no hope ever to get the World Council of Churches or ecumenical leaders to recognize the Pentecostal revival. I am not anxious for a recognition of Pentecostals, but I am keenly desirous for a recognition of the Pentecostal experience, and I pray that the Holy Spirit himself will move into the churches and have His rightful place in the lives of the ministry and membership. (See page 107.)

In Pentecostal circles we strive to maintain the emphasis on the work of the Holy Spirit, because the Church of the New Testament had no other claim. They had no rich libraries as we have today. They had to depend on the Holy Spirit and His teaching and guidance. They had no other option but to minister, to preach, and to write under the inspiration of the Holy Spirit. In nearly two thousand years no one has yet come up with any writings that can compare with the New Testament in stirring the lives of men and women who will read it, or inspiring those who will preach it.

Jesus said, "I will pray the Father, and he shall give you another Comforter, that he may abide with you for ever.... Ye know him; for he dwelleth with you, and shall be in you" (John 14:16, 17). He further promised: "And, lo, I am with you alway, even unto the end of the world" (Matt. 28:20). Why is it then that we do not have more evidence of the work of the Spirit in the Church today? I think I can see His work in many places and cases where others have failed to recognize Him because they attribute His work to other influences or to their own efforts. In spite of this He is constantly at work raising up men in the Church with special ministries.

The ministry in the Church is of tremendous importance. I shall never forget years ago when I read the 4th chapter of the book of Ephesians. I came to the 8th verse which said: "He led captivity captive, and gave gifts unto men." Immediately I thought of the gifts of the Spirit. But when I came to the 11th verse I read: "And he *gave* some, apostles; and some, prophets; and some, evangelists; and some, pastors and teachers; for the perfecting of the saints." That is where many stop and then seek perfect saints. But I believe it means that Christ gave these ministries that by them the saints may be trained or perfected, or matured "for the work of the ministry [by all saints in the church], for the edifying of the body of Christ." When I check with I Corinthians 12:28, I find that "God hath *set* some in the church, first apostles, secondarily prophets, thirdly teachers," etc. These were not gifts of the Spirit; they were ministries given by Christ and set by God.

When I realized all this I asked myself, "Did Christ give me a ministry gift? Has God set me in the Church for any particular ministry?" From that time on I have been less concerned about my career and more about the ministry. Am I doing the will of God? Am I obedient to the guidance of the Holy Spirit? Am I perfecting the saints that they may be able to build the Church? No longer did I look for the gifts of the Spirit. I knew that if I would be faithful in the ministry, the Holy Spirit would manifest His gifts through me that I might bring them to the saints for their edification.

Now let us stop in the 12th chapter of I Corinthians for a while. In a retreat with a score or more of theologians and ecumenical leaders in 1956, I dealt with this matter. I gave my personal testimony of how the Lord had blessed me, and that I had seen a manifestation of all the gifts of the Spirit at one time or another in my ministry. Then Dr. Henry P. van Dusen asked me "How can we get those gifts?" I replied: "Gentlemen, it is not a question of seeking for gifts, but rather a matter of receiving the Giver of these gifts." Once you have the Spirit, and the Spirit has full control of you, the gifts will follow or be manifested by the Spirit through you.

I know the general idea is that the Holy Spirit gives certain gifts to certain men and thus enables them to do specific things. There is a sense in which this is true, but it is not true that He gives any man a gift that he may use. No man can *use* the Holy

Spirit, but rather the Holy Spirit uses the man as His channel to manifest His gifts to the Church. The key to the entire operation is found in the 7th verse: "But the *manifestation* of the Spirit is given to every man to profit withal." It is the manifestation that is most important.

Reading from the King James Version, I would put it this way: "For to one [in a specific assembly of the church] is given by the Spirit [here I add: the manifestation of] the word of wisdom; to another [the manifestation of] the word of knowledge by the same Spirit." All the nine so-called gifts of the Spirit are first manifestations in the life of some member in the Assembly, and are thus passed on to the others as gifts of the Spirit. *All* may have occasional manifestation of *all* the gifts, but some have more frequent manifestations of the same gift, and thus we have the ministries which are listed in verse 28. Verse 29 only emphasizes the fact that all have not the same ministry, nor even do all have ministries, but the fact still remains that "the manifestation of the Spirit is given to every man."

During the past fifty years these three chapters, or shall I say four (11, 12, 13 and 14), in I Corinthians have been of the greatest importance to the Pentecostal people. Without them we would have had chaotic conditions. It seems that Paul knew exactly what was happening among us and wrote very carefully about what to do and what to expect. Untold times I have had the great privilege to behold or enjoy all these wonderful manifestations of the Spirit. It is indeed a thrill to be in a meeting where the Spirit moves upon the assembled disciples.

I am happy to tell you that you no longer have to go to a Pentecostal Assembly to see and hear such manifestations. There are many churches outside the Pentecostal Movement here in the States where you will find all the manifestations of the Spirit. The Holy Spirit is indeed finding recognition and His rightful place in the established historic churches. I think I am privileged to enjoy this more than anyone else. I have seen the Spirit at work in Presbyterian, Episcopal, Methodist, Baptist, and other churches. There is absolutely no difference between what I observe in these renewed churches now and what I have experienced in Pentecostal Assemblies of the past forty years.

Recently at Central Bible Institute in Springfield, Missouri, one of the instructors said to me: "You seem to have discovered a new dimension to this Pentecostal experience in revival." With a happy smile, I replied: "Yes, when I got out of my Pentecostal shell, I found the Holy Spirit was at work in other churches all over the world with the same blessing and the same manifestations."

Shall I describe to you a truly Pentecostal service in a Presbyterian church where a Princeton Seminary graduate is the pastor? This is what happened there. After the second hymn someone began to speak with tongues. I knew it was not a devotional prayer. Prayers in the Spirit are seldom interpreted. But this was clearly a "gift" or "message" (I do not like this unscriptural term) to the gathering. How did I know? Discernment of spirits enables you to know what is in the mind of the Spirit and what is happening. So I knew in this case that an interpretation by the Spirit must follow. I prayed, as Paul teaches us, for the interpretation. I have often given interpretation of tongues, but I do not consider myself an interpreter. However, I always tell the Spirit I am ready when He wills to use me. I was still praying when the pastor gave the interpretation. It was beautiful, thrilling and inspiring. It blessed my soul to hear a Princeton Seminary graduate so full of the Spirit that he could give interpretation to an utterance of the Holy Spirit with tongues. After this interpretation there was a deep devotional and worshipful atmosphere in the chapel. All prayed softly.

While this was going on, my mind went back to the night two years earlier when I first met this pastor, shortly after he had received the baptism in the Spirit. I pleaded with him then not to leave his church or resign from the professorship in a nearby seminary. I advised him to remain humble, loving, kind, and gentle, and to take all the bumps and kicks that might come his way. How glad I was now that I had told him to stay where he was until God called him away or somebody pushed him out so hard that he could not remain there. But, thank God, he is still there.

Now back to that meeting. They sang a worshipful chorus to bring us all back to earth, for it seemed heaven had opened above us. I saw tears of joy. The love of God frequently moves us to tears. Call it emotionalism if you like, but I would rather see people, any time, weep for sheer joy in the Holy Ghost than to see them weeping in a theater because of some "make-believe" show. I fear we are so afraid of emotionalism that we have caused people to give expression to their feelings (and they seek for this expression) in amusement centers. What an ungodly people we are when we do not get edification by the Spirit in the Church.

The next moment the pastor had a manifestation of prophecy by the Spirit. And what a gift it was to the congregation! Again I was thrilled to find here, in a Presbyterian church, the very same manifestations of the Spirit that I had enjoyed among many nations, in many countries, and now among many denominations. The meeting that night continued to be just one glorious manifestation of the Spirit after another, till we had tongues and interpretation, prophecy, discernment of spirits, gifts of healing to the sick, the word of knowledge, and the word of wisdom. Finally it was a *miracle* to find all this happening in a Presbyterian church.

Now if you were to challenge me today and tell me that you know of Pentecostal churches where they do not have these manifestations in the way I have described them here, I will have to admit that I see a tendency among our people to go the way others have gone. Gradually we are preaching more and more doctrine and have less and less demonstration of the power of the Spirit. It is a great tragedy when the Spirit becomes "a displaced person" in the Church, and all kinds of substitutes are introduced. In order to explain how or why the Holy Spirit had been displaced in the churches at various times in the history of Christianity, let me conclude by telling you about the experience I recently had when God spoke to me by the Spirit and in an audible voice said: "God has no grandsons." (See pages 61 to 68 for this story.)

Missions Lecture III

THE HOLY SPIRIT IN THE MISSION OF THE CHURCH

This being the last of these Missions Lectures, I would like to take this opportunity to express my sincere appreciation to President McCord and the faculty and the students for the kind reception I have enjoyed here and for the cordial attitude of everyone I have met on the campus. Were it not for the urgent call to Union Theological Seminary in New York, I would have loved to stay on here. I trust the blessing of the Lord will continue to increase as the years go by.

If any of you have become disturbed by what I have said thus far, then I am encouraged by what Dr. Henry P. van Dusen wrote recently in the *United Church Herald*: "The Holy Spirit has always been troublesome to Church officialdom, because He does seem to be unruly, unpredictable, and radical." In 1955 he wrote: "The call to the ministry is to be alert to discern every movement of the living, confounding, uncontrollable Spirit of God, in what someone has called 'His Sovereign Unpredictability.'"

I am so happy to know that there are those in the Ecumenical Movement who realize that to expect a move of the Holy Spirit to be desirable by all and to be according to faith and order *without any ardor* is no longer possible. Many have been convinced that to welcome the ardor that the Holy Spirit creates will disturb much of the order that we have established.

According to our Scripture reading in the Acts it was clear that from the very beginning the motivating power of the Church was the Holy Spirit. We read: "They that were scattered abroad went everywhere preaching the word." Who was scattered abroad? All except the apostles. In the first century all church members were scattered abroad, and the Church was the mission; today the church stays home and the apostles are scattered abroad to be missionaries. It is all in reverse now. I do not think we have much hope of "turning the world upside down" if we continue to send out the apostles (missionaries) while the Church stays peacefully at home. It was the method of "every-member evangelism" that did the miracle in apostolic days. But you can hardly call this a method, for no one had devised any system as yet. It was simply the strategy of the Holy Spirit, for He was supreme Executive in the Church. I have discovered in my own ministry that the Holy Spirit never develops a monotonous even course of action. In every instance He has a peculiar way of meeting the need of the individual, of the church, of the community, of the nation.

The Holy Spirit, in His sovereign unpredictability, gives different guidance for every occasion. The early Church, in absolute obedience to Him, went along with this. So we find Philip, one of the deacons, now scattered with the rest of the Church, preaching in Samaria. The man that was elected to take care of finances suddenly became a revivalist. Or would we call him a missionary? Today, we have an organized officialdom, and everyone must work according to the organization's dictates. The missionary has his board and they allocate his field. He must study the Theology of Missions, even if he has no knowledge of the Holy Spirit.

In the Acts of the Apostles we find that they "went everywhere preaching the word." This was the one thing that no one failed to do. There was no question of ordination here. It was only a question of being filled with the Spirit and finding an opportunity to witness. "But," someone says, "they had persecution." Yes, and a great religious leader, Saul of Tarsus, was the chief persecutor. "He made havoc of the church," but the more he maltreated them, the more they extended their operations, and the Church grew by the power of the Holy Spirit. He could not stop the Church, but the Lord soon stopped him. I am sure they prayed for deliverance from this cruel oppressor. Some day when we walk the streets of gold, I would like to ask those saints how they prayed.

They might have had in mind that the Lord should let him die. I can hardly think they prayed for his conversion, because when it happened they could not believe it, and for years he was not accepted.

Saul was the ringleader of the mob that stoned Stephen. This was another deacon who had become a mighty preacher, not because of election or appointment by the Church, but because of the ministry that Christ gave and for which God had set him in the Church. Stephen faithfully followed his Master and prayed, "Father, forgive them." This prayer God answered. He forgave Saul of Tarsus, and laid upon him the burden of the ministry that Stephen had. To do so the Lord arrested him on the way to Damascus. The "old man," Saul of Tarsus, died and a "new creature," Paul the Apostle, was born of the Spirit.

Under the ministry of a humble, rather unknown disciple in Damascus, Paul received the Holy Spirit. No longer did he give orders. He now took orders from the Holy Spirit. He could not even return to visit his converts in places where he had ministered with such success. Why not? He was "forbidden of the Holy Spirit," and when he decided to choose another direction, "the Spirit suffered him not." The Holy Spirit was the strategist in the Church. He wanted to reach the whole world. He was moving upon all flesh. He was seeking men who would yield to Him so that He could manifest himself through them and by mighty works and miracles bring men and women to Christ.

We are thinking of the Spirit in the world. We have already seen the great change He brought about by breaking the racial barrier in the house of Cornelius. Now we come to the time when He broke the geographical barrier. The Gospel must go beyond the boundaries of Asia. Paul heard the now-famous Macedonian Call. This changed the course of his ministry and the course of the Christian Church, and for that matter, the course of history. There was no question of the Church and missions; it was the Church in action everywhere, or should I say the Holy Spirit in action through the Church. When a Spirit-filled community goes into action, it is all mission and all Church.

Paul and Silas came to Europe by a revelation of the Spirit. There was no church there. They could not even find the Macedonian man. They did not waste time looking for him. They just preached to the first crowd they found on the banks of the river. Soon they were arrested and thrown in prison with their backs beaten. I can imagine Silas asking Paul whether he had a real vision from the Spirit. Was he sure the Lord had brought them here? Let me assure you that guidance by the Spirit is no guarantee that you will escape all trials and troubles. He makes no detours; He takes us right through. Rather than complaining or questioning their guidance or the wisdom of God, the two prisoners acted like free men and began to sing in the night. They sang up an earthquake. The prison doors opened. The jailer and his household were saved. How thrilling it is to work with God.

In that generation when all this happened, there was universal corruption. Every precept of the moral law was violated. The standard of conscience was at a very low ebb. In such a world the Church of Christ was born. Yet the disciples had no wealth, no social position, no prestige, no government aid, and no help

om any established institutions. They were in themselves a
espised and feeble folk, without influence, without skill, without
ducation, without a New Testament or even an Old Testament,
es, without any literature to place in the hands of people. They
d not even have a single Christian house of worship. Powers,
istoms, and public sentiment were all against them. They were
eproached, reviled, persecuted, and subjected to exile and death.
ut those early Christians had the *indwelling power of the Holy
pirit*. With this unique equipment, they faced a hostile world
id all the malignant powers of darkness. They conquered, and
ithin seventy years, according to the smallest estimate, there
ere half a million followers of Jesus Christ. In other words,
ith the power of the Holy Spirit upon the Church, she increased
membership more than four thousandfold in three-score years.

Please believe that what I am going to say now is not
pasting. I am simply witnessing to the facts as they are for the
ory of God in recognition of the power of the Holy Spirit. Much
ie same story as that recorded in the Acts can be written about
ie Pentecostal Movement of the 20th century. In the beginning
eryone who received the baptism seemed to be going somewhere
p tell about it. Some began to go to foreign lands. They could not
e called missionaries, for there were no "sending" churches. They
id a call from the Spirit but no mission from the Church. They
id to venture into unknown fields and live dangerously. They had
p live by faith and trust God for everything.

In this way two men with their familes came from Amer-
a to my homeland, South Africa, to tell us that we could receive
ie baptism in the Holy Spirit on the same pattern as the Apostles
id. There was quite a bit of spiritual life in the Reformed church-
s because of the ministry of that great man of God, Dr. Andrew
turray. His meetings and writings had produced a wonderful
evival for deepening of spiritual life, sanctification, and divine
ealing of the sick. When his followers heard that there was an
ven greater blessing than his deep teaching on the life and work
f the Spirit, they came to investigate.

The American preachers were holding meetings in an old
resbyterian church on Bree Street in Johannesburg. The 600-seat
uditorium was packed every night of the week for almost eight-
en months. Men of every nation in that wicked "gold center"

came to these services to see the miracles that the Holy Spirit wa
doing. Crutches and canes and all kinds of gadgets from broke
and sick bodies were left on the platform in a heap. These wer
not healing meetings; but sin and sickness are the two main prob
lems of mankind, and here they found deliverance from bot
Many drunkards got converted and then brought their companion
back to be changed by the power of the Lord.

One of Dr. Andrew Murray's first students and also first mi
sionaries from his church in Wellington, Cape Province, was Piete
Louis le Roux. I worked very closely with him from 1931 to 194
I loved to hear him tell of the gracious ministry of Dr. Murra
whom he loved and appreciated very much. He told me how h
came to investigate this amazing new revival in Johannesbur
When he saw and heard sinners weeping, the sick who were heale
laughing, and those who were filled with the Spirit praying i
tongues and singing, he turned away in disgust at all this mixe
noise. This was no proper order. He had been reared and traine
as a Dutch Reformed Church member and missionary. He cou'
never accept these uncouth services as the work of the Hol
Spirit. Thoroughly disgusted and deeply disappointed, he decide
to go back to his field of labor. On the train he began to try an
figure things out. What should he tell his friends? What was th
outstanding characteristic of all that he had witnessed in thos
meetings? Was there anything good and kind, yet absolutel
truthful, that he could say? Then he remembered that he ha
never in his life met people who were more in love with Jesu
and were more excited about the living Christ who had becom
so real to them in these Holy Ghost meetings. He had never bee
in a church where Christ was more magnified, glorified, and wo
shipped than here. They seemed to be talking about Jesus all th
time and seldom mentioned the Holy Spirit unless it was to sa
that Jesus had baptized them in the Spirit. No evil spirit woul
do those things. Then after all, this must be the work of the Hol
Spirit.

At the nearest station he got off the train and took the ne
train back to those noisy meetings. He never left again. He be
came president of the movement, known as the Apostolic Fait
Mission of South Africa, and served in that capacity until 194
I never knew a more perfect man than P. L. le Roux. Dr. Andre

urray's ministry had made an indelible impression upon him.
nder such leadership the work in South Africa thrived until
day it has become one of the strongest Christian and missionary
cieties of the land.

I can keep you busy for hours, telling about marvels and
iracles that I have seen in South Africa. But I must speak of
e work of the Holy Spirit in the whole world. So let me tell you
a country that I visited recently. In Brazil, South America, there
one of the largest Pentecostal movements in the world. This
so began about fifty years ago when two Scandinavian-Americans
lt called to Brazil. No mission board sent them. They went in
ind faith—very foolish according to present-day standards—but
ey simply kept telling that Jesus was the Saviour, Healer, mighty
aptizer, and the soon-coming King. Before long, miracles
healing took place. This caused the conversion of many Bra-
lians. Then the new converts began to tell and to pray for oth-
s. More miracles followed and soon the Gospel reached the
terior until all through the land, Assemblies of God were estab-
shed. Now there is a movement with about fifteen hundred
nurches and a community of about a quarter of a million.

I must point out, however, that this is not the only Pentecos-
l work in Brazil. About the same time that the Scandinavian
ethren came there, an Italian-American brother from Chicago
d also heard the call. He went all alone and knew nothing about
e others. He commenced with one soul and then one family and
en one congregation. Today there are about fifteen hundred of
ese Christian congregations with a community also of a quarter
a million. These two movements have different ideas about
nurch government and they have no understanding nor fellow-
ip with one another thus far.

Besides these two great movements in Brazil, there are now
any other smaller works and a number of large independent
nurches. Those who live in that land assure me that a third
roup could be as strong as the two first mentioned. That
ould mean that there is a Pentecostal community of close to
ree-quarters of a million people in Brazil. Leaders from other
nurches assure me that this is a very conservative estimate. They
ink it quite possible that there may now be at least a million
entecostals.

Many of you will have heard about the wonderful work Chile. The strange thing about this revival is that it was a Meth dist leader who came from the States, where he received th Pentecostal experience that introduced his people to this blessin Whereas most Pentecostals practice believers' baptism by imme sion, this movement remained Methodist in both doctrine ar church government and still practice infant baptism. They wer taught to be extremely exclusive, and developed a strong isol tionism that has caused serious weakness in the Movement. Aft the death of the American leader, the work was taken over b nationals, and several splits resulted. Nevertheless, the enti Movement has enjoyed a phenomenal growth, and it has becon one of the strongest Christian influences in the country. In r cent years some strong Assemblies of God and other church have come into existence in Chile. In a few exceptional cases the have all cooperated in great campaigns of mass-evangelism. I a hoping that this will eventually develop into a more perpetu Pentecostal fellowship.

Another remarkable modern-day Pentecostal revival is four in Italy. Many have thought this is the last place where it wou be possible to establish a strong Pentecostal church. During or of my visits to Rome I spoke to leaders of the Waldensian Churc They told me that they had been busy in Italy for centuries ar had made very little progress. They said that in forty years tl Pentecostal Movement had grown more than the Waldensia had in four centuries. I have had the privilege of enjoying son very remarkable experiences in Italy during the days when the was much persecution. I saw them worshipping in dark, din basements that were overcrowded. After the Second World Wa hundreds of little assemblies sprang up like mushrooms all ove the country. Finally, under the new constitution the courts gav the Movement recognition and liberty. Today there is a good Bib school and many well-built churches.

I must draw your attention to one outstanding fact about tl work in Italy. They have never had any mass-meetings. This wa outlawed. In fact many were jailed for having house-gathering Actually the work thrived by personal witnessing—each-one-te one. Here again is proof that the Holy Spirit never has to stic to the same methods or principles of evangelism. When He work any method will succeed, because it is never the technique but the power of the Spirit that insures success.

When I think of this, I cannot agree with the idea that the Church in China and other countries behind the "curtains" have gone out of existence. They may have been driven underground like in the days of the catacombs, but the Church annihilated? No, sir, I cannot believe that. The gates of hell shall not prevail against her. The Holy Spirit is at work even where every missionary has been ousted. Persecution will not stop the revival. On the contrary, it often vitalizes the Church.

Now let us turn our attention to the Congo, in Central Africa, for a few moments. In 1914 two young men from England, William Burton and James Salter, felt the call to this land. They had to learn the language from the children because the older folk ran away from the white men. So in learning from the children, they also taught the children. From the very beginning then they opened schools, which was rather unusual in those days. Very few of our missionaries bothered about an educational program. Today it is different and there are schools everywhere. In the Congo these early schools proved to be another wonderful strategy of the Holy Spirit. He knows the end from the beginning and He plans accordingly.

In recent years a great and unprecedented revival has broken out. Yes, we now have revivals on top of Pentecostal revivals, and they are wonderful indeed. This new revival in the Congo commenced one day in a school where the teacher tried to explain the love of God to the children. The Holy Spirit was at work. The teacher was overwhelmed by the love of God and began to weep. The children began to weep. Suddenly they realized that their parents whom they loved did not know the love of God. They ran from school and pleaded with their loved ones to accept Jesus, the Son of God, who loved them and had died for them. What the missionary had failed to accomplish by preaching, the children now succeeded in doing by witnessing. This revival spread from school to school through the jungles. At the last count, I heard that 506 new churches had been opened in eighteen months. Where do you find 506 pastors in so short a period? The Holy Spirit had taken care of that when He led the missionaries to start with schools. The main textbook in all the schools has been the Bible.

Now the first students were grown and married, and there was room for their ministry.

That was in the Congo. But every land has a different story to tell. In all my travels I have never found a universal method, a general technique, or an acknowledged system by which the Holy Spirit works. He has glorious variety, but there is one rule to remember—always let Him do it. Let the Spirit manifest His gifts.

In conclusion, let me say that nothing less than a knowledge of the Holy Spirit comparable to that actually portrayed on the pages of the New Testament would have fulfilled the Lord's promises concerning the Comforter whose coming was to make His own departure expedient. He told His disciples: "It is expedient for you that I go away: for if I go not away, the Comforter will not come unto you." On the day of Pentecost the Comforter came and did those very things that Jesus had said He would do. Now the disciples knew the Lord had been glorified, and according to John 7:37, 38 rivers of living water were flowing from their innermost beings. They were still natural enough in the essentials of human nature. They had their full share of human weaknesses, but for all that, there was a constant blending of the supernatural with the natural. There was a victorious ring about everything in spite of bitter persecution. God was with them. God was in them. Indeed, the Comforter had come.

In contrast to all that is the vagueness that spreads over nearly all modern doctrine and experience of the Holy Spirit among Christians. It can scarcely be otherwise when the baptism in the Holy Spirit is either denied as a spiritual crisis for the believer, or else kept as a blessing to be appropriated simply by faith, along with a warning against emotionalism. True and splendid things are being said and written by Christian leaders of our day, but when the supreme problem of the churches is the powerlessness of their members, little will be accomplished until the membership is truly revived. We need an every-member salvation, followed by an every-member baptism in the Spirit which will produce an every-member evangelism that will again turn the world upside down

GOD HAS NO GRANDSONS

It was early morning, around four o'clock, in the month of January. There was snow everywhere outside. Radio news had predicted 10 degrees below zero temperature that night. I was awakened from a deep restful sleep by a voice that seemed loud and clear. I sat up in my bed and looked around the room. The street light was shining through one window. I saw no one in the room. All was quiet, yet that voice kept ringing in my ear. It seemed I could still hear it distinctly saying: "God has no grandsons."

Perhaps I had left the radio on. I leaned over and felt the set; it was ice cold. The thought struck me that even the radio must be warm before it can say anything. Cold Christians have nothing to say. But where did that voice come from? Who spoke those words? I kept listening, but there was only the sound of heavy breathing from those sleeping in the next rooms. Then it seemed as if there was someone in my room and the presence made me feel good. Suddenly it dawned on me. It must be the Holy Spirit who spoke to me. But why should He say those words to me? What does He mean?—*God has no grandsons.*

I snapped on the light and took my Bible. Is there a text about any "grandsons"? I could remember none. "How about sons?" I turned to the Gospel of John, chapter one, verses 12 and 13. "But as many as received him, to them gave he power to become the sons of God, even to them that believe on his name: which were born, not of blood, nor of the will of the flesh, nor of the will of man, *but of God.*"

I checked further Scriptures. Romans 8:14, "For as many as are led by the Spirit of God, they are the sons of God." I John 3:1, 2, "Behold, what manner of love the Father hath bestowed upon us, that we should be called the sons of God. . . . Beloved, now are we the sons of God." Galatians 4:4–7, "God sent forth his son...to redeem them that were under the law, that we might receive the adoption of sons. And because ye are sons, God hath sent forth the Spirit of his Son into your hearts, crying, Abba, Father. Wherefore, thou art no more a servant, but a son; and if a son, then an heir of God through Christ."

I could find nothing about grandsons.

Then I began to check whether there was any text that might signify that God could be the grandfather of anyone, but I could find nothing in the Old or New Testament. So I concluded: "God is nobody's grandfather."

It was about five in the morning. I switched off the light and put on my "thinking cap." What had I discovered? Nothing new. I always knew God is our Father in heaven. He is the Father of all believers, and believers in Christ are called sons of God. So what? I had only found a new way of saying an old truth. God has no grandsons, only sons. God is nobody's grandfather, only Father.

At breakfast that morning I discussed this experience with the pastor and his wife. The voice and the thought seemed to stay with me all the time. This lasted for all the ten days that I continued to minister in Minneapolis, Minnesota. I received no revelation or inspiration. Those who I talked to thought it was a very peculiar way of saying that only those who are born of God are sons of God. Beyond that there is no relationship. God has no grandsons. He is no grandfather.

I had to fly to Chicago and by phone made reservations on an evening flight. I never checked just how that flight would go. After we were airborne I discovered we had to change planes in Milwaukee. I was a little displeased because it was another bitter cold night with below zero temperatures. Then the "still small voice" whispered: "Maybe you should meet someone on this trip to speak to." That settled it. I was watching and seeking to find that "someone." I looked over the passengers in the plane. This gave me no guidance. Then after landing I looked over the people in the terminal at Milwaukee. No one spoke to me and I saw none that I felt led to speak to.

Then came the call for the flight to Chicago. When I came to the gate, I was all alone, the only passenger. I felt terribly lonely and very homesick. Then I heard voices. I saw five men in black come toward me. They began to shake hands with each other, and only one came on toward the gate. The others waved farewell. So it seemed we were the only two passengers for the flight. Maybe this was the person whom I should talk to. There was no one else, so why not get acquainted?

"Are you a passenger to Chicago?" I asked. "Yes, sir. Are we the only passengers?" said my friend. "There is the last call, and it seems we must be the only passengers. Are you an R.C. priest, sir?" I questioned. "Yes, I am a priest with an educational appointment," came his reply as we walked to the plane. Then he asked: "And you, what are you?" "Oh, I am also a priest." I said. "But what kind of priest are you?" queried my companion. "Sir, I am a Pentecostal priest," said I. "You mean you belong to the Movement that is growing so fast around the world?" "Yes, sir, that is what is generally admitted these days." "Could you tell me about them? Do you know much about the Pentecostal Movement?" I told him that I had been in the Movement since 1918 and that I had served as secretary for several world conferences. "Oh, how fortunate I am to meet you," he exclaimed as we boarded the plane. "I have been hoping to meet with someone who could tell me all about the Pentecostalists."

As we took two seats, side-by-side, the stewardess offered her services, and my friend said to her: "Lady, we need nothing. We only want to talk. So you may go to the front seat and crawl up and go to sleep." When he said this the Holy Spirit spoke to me and said, "Tell him that God has no grandsons." Then I knew that now I would receive further revelation on the word that I heard in the early morning.

I began to witness about my conversion when I was born again—born of God. I continued to relate how after my conversion in 1916 I had received the Holy Spirit in 1918, and how I was called into the ministry. I kept quoting New Testament parallels, first saying, "Christ was born of the Spirit, which we call the Virgin Birth. Then at the age of thirty, at Jordan, He received the Holy Spirit—two distinct happenings. First there was birth, then enduement for service. Christ never ministered until He had received the Holy Spirit. So Christ commanded His disciples not to leave the city of Jerusalem until they had received the Holy

Spirit. On the day of Pentecost He came. That is why we are called Pentecostals. Later in Samaria they had been baptized and had enjoyed miracles, but after that the Apostles came from Jerusalem and only then did they receive the Holy Spirit. Again two experiences. Cornelius had a life of prayer and angels appeared to him. He already had experienced the grace of God, but when Peter preached to him he also received the Holy Spirit, and we speak of that incident as the Gentile Pentecost."

Suddenly my friend interrupted with: "Oh, I see what you are trying to do. You are trying to revive the Apostolic Church of the New Testament in this century, and you expect the same things to happen now that were experienced by the early churches."

"No, sir," I replied. "We are trying nothing of the kind. We are only standing back and watching it happen all over the world. The first church was a creation of the Holy Spirit, and He has not changed; but in every generation He wants to repeat what He did in the first Christian Church through the first leaders and members."

Then I proceeded to tell him how in miracle fashion, in many countries almost simultaneously at the turn of this century, the Holy Spirit moved upon those who were praying for revival. This happened in the United States, Europe, Asia, and Africa—on every continent and in almost every country of the world. The Pentecostal revival became known as the Pentecostal Movement which now has somewhere around ten million adherents. I have no time and space to give all the details here of what I told my friend that night.

Finally he interrupted me again and said: "I take it that you think all the other Christian churches are wrong or they have gone wrong?"

I prayed for guidance to answer this question. In a flash I got it. "Yes, sir, they have all gone wrong, and even now the Pentecostals are falling into the same ditch and they are going wrong too."

He looked shocked. "But what do they do? When, why, where, how do they all go wrong?"

"Now, sir," I said, "your church claims to be the oldest church. Is that not so?" "Yes, there you are right," he answered.

"Then your church went wrong first, and after that all fell into the same rut or ditch." I added, "They all do the same thing—they begin right and keep right for a long time and then they go off the highway of God into the by-ways of men."

"What do they do? Please tell me quick. I must know this before we get off at Chicago and have to part." My friend seemed very anxious.

With a deep prayer in my heart I said to him in slow, clear words: "They give God grandsons, and *God has no grandsons.*" Almost dumbfounded he said, "I have never heard of such a thing! Grandsons? What do you mean?"

I answered him, "Actually I never heard of such a thing until a few weeks ago when I heard an audible voice say to me, 'God has no grandsons'; and only now, this very moment, have I learned what the words mean. Now I shall try to explain why, where, when, and how all this happens.

"John the Baptist preached, 'Repent ye, for the kingdom of heaven is at hand.' Then Jesus preached, 'Repent, for the kingdom of heaven is at hand.' On the day of Pentecost, Peter preached: 'Repent...and ye shall receive the gift of the Holy Ghost. For the promise is unto you, and to your children, and to all that are afar off, even as many as the Lord our God shall call.' In the house of Cornelius, Peter told the Gentiles: 'Whosoever believeth in him shall receive remission of sins.' Thus it was clear that every Jew and every Gentile that came into the Christian Church did so by repentance, or conversion, or being born of the Spirit. Every one had a very definite encounter with the living Christ, the resurrected Son of God. The record in Acts also shows that they received the Holy Spirit. Of this Paul was so sure that when he met the disciples at Ephesus he asked them: 'Have ye received the Holy Ghost since ye believed?'

"This revival continued and the Church grew and Christianity swept the world of that time. Then some Jew or some Gentile began to reason: 'I was a Jew [or Gentile] and became a Christian by repentance of sin and conversion from Judaism [or paganism] and so was my wife; but this boy of mine has never been a Jew [or Gentile]. He did not grow up in the temple. He was born from Christian parents, in a Christian home, and was brought up in the Christian Church. He is *born* Christian.'

"Now this may all be true, but he has never been born of the Spirit, and that child has not repented as a sinner because he has had a strict training as the son of Christian parents. He was taught to try and live like a Christian, for he is the son of God's children.

"The nicest thing you could say about him is that being the son of two of God's children who became a son and a daughter of God by regeneration, he is now a grandson of God—but there it is, *God has no grandsons.*

"Gradually the early Christians began to accept as members into their churches their well-trained but unregenerated children until the pews were packed with members who had no encounter with Christ as Saviour and much less a Pentecostal experience. They were not born of the Spirit and therefore could not be filled with the Spirit. God says: '[It is] not by might nor by power but by my Spirit.' The Spirit found no more blood-cleansed hearts in the Church to dwell in, and the Church cooled off spiritually until even in the pulpit there stood well-trained but unregenerated preachers who spoke the letter but had not the Spirit.

"When Emperor Constantine caused his army to be baptized into the Church, she was already so dead with a generation of unregenerated grandsons that these sinful soldiers felt quite at home in the Christian society. Spiritually the Church was dead. But God did not leave it at that. Time and again the Holy Spirit found a heart through which He could reach the ears of the people. Such men were the exception and were looked upon as fanatics and usually were persecuted or martyred.

"There came, for instance, the man known as Martin Luther. Out of his ministry came the Reformation. There seemed to come into life a new church with membership that had a fresh and very real encounter with Christ and with the Holy Spirit. However, it was not long before some Lutheran parents began to reason and say, 'But our children have never been Roman Catholics; they are just born Lutherans.' Right there it began again—grandsons for God in the Lutheran or Reformation churches.

"Then came John Wesley in England, and we had the Western revivals. Again men and women were challenged to seek God and be born of the Spirit. But after two or three generations some parents began to reason: 'Our children have never been Anglicans, or Lutherans, or Roman Catholics; why they are just born Wesleyans or Methodists.' Soon the grandsons filled the churches and the revival was over.

"Now at the turn of this century came the Pentecostal revival. All were called to repentance. Everyone who was born of the Spirit was now encouraged to seek and receive the baptism in the Spirit with the New Testament evidence of speaking in tongues and with the manifestations of the Holy Spirit, such as prophecy and healing. No matter how the older churches objected, the revival spread. It was the same in the Catholic countries as in Protestant countries and in pagan lands. When people are born of the Spirit they *live.* When such people are filled with the Spirit, they receive power to become witnesses.

"But what is happening now? We find that in the beginning of this revival, fifty years ago, everyone was expected to be filled with the Spirit with the confirmation of 'tongues' before they could hold any office in the Pentecostal church or the Pentecostal Assembly, but there are today the sons and grandsons of Pentecostal pioneers who are teaching in Sunday schools and are holding all kinds of offices in the local churches without ever having had a real baptism in the Spirit according to Acts 2:4. The waves of Pentecostal power and revival are receding fast. There is danger that in another generation we may have a Pentecostal Movement without Pentecost—that is, without the experience, just like other revivals which still emphasize some or other *truth* but never experience it. Revivals crystalize into societies and establish churches when the 'grandsons' take over. But *God has no grandsons.*"

"Shocking...shocking...," was all my friend the priest could say at first. Then he suggested that we might meet again some time. "Your grandfather story has upset my philosophy," he concluded. We parted with a warm handshake, and we have not met again, but I prayed for him. I wonder whether he pondered that evening: "What am I? A son or a grandson?" Then the next morning when he prayed, did he remember " 'Our Father, which art in heaven'? Is God my Father? Have I treated Him like a grandfather? But God is no one's grandfather." I often wonder what he will tell me if we should meet again.

I have repeated the above experience almost weekly since 1959. I have related it to meetings of ministers, to the faculty members of seminaries, to students in seminaries, and to so many theologians that I cannot remember their number or names. Again and again I have been asked to write the story, and at the request of some leading Protestant churchmen, I do so with the prayer that this message might stir honest men and women all the way from Roman Catholic churches to the Protestant churches and even to the ranks of my own Pentecostal brethren everywhere.

REMEMBER...GOD HAS NO GRANDSONS!

(The foregoing may be obtained as a free tract from the writer.)

THE BAPTISM IN THE HOLY SPIRIT

Often the question is asked: Why say "the baptism"? It is because I consider it the best theological term. The very idea originated from heaven. "The baptism of John, was it from heaven, or of men?" (Luke 20:4). "He that sent me to *baptize* with water, the same said unto me, Upon whom thou shalt see the Spirit descending, and remaining on him, the same is he which *baptizeth* with the Holy Ghost" (John 1:33).

John the Baptist also said: "Behold the Lamb of God, which taketh away the sin of the world" (John 1:29). It seems clear that John emphasized that Jesus would have two special ministries. As the Lamb of God on Calvary He would become the Saviour, and as the one upon whom the Spirit remains, He would become the baptizer on the day of Pentecost. "Jesus Christ the same yesterday, and to day, and for ever" (Heb. 13:8). He still saves from sin and He still baptizes in the Holy Spirit.

God gave the word "baptism" to John, and also the image of the act. "I indeed baptize with water. . . . He shall baptize you with the Holy Ghost" (Matt. 3:11). Jesus confirmed this when He said: "For John truly baptized with water; but ye shall be baptized with the Holy Ghost not many days hence" (Acts 1:5). Thus Christ commenced His ministry of baptizing in the Holy Spirit on the day of Pentecost. This was the first time that any followers of Christ were baptized in the Spirit by Him.

About ten years later Peter still declared that Christ was the baptizer in the Spirit. In his defense, before the other apostles in Jerusalem, for accepting and baptizing the Gentiles in the house of Cornelius into the church, he said: "Then remembered I the word of the Lord, how that he said, John indeed baptized with water; but ye shall be baptized with the Holy Ghost" (Acts 11:16). He denied any responsibility for what happened to the Gentiles. He declared that Christ had first baptized them in the Holy Spirit, and so he dared not refuse to have them baptized in water and thus acknowledge them as members of the body of Christ.

The Baptism of the Spirit

Much of the confusion today is a matter of semantics. All too often we hear people talk about the baptism *of* the Spirit when they mean *in* or with. The baptism *of* the Spirit comes at conversion or regeneration. People of the world cannot receive the Spirit (John 14:17), but He will reprove the world of sin (John 16:9) and of righteousness, bringing them to Christ (I Cor. 1:30) to be redeemed of sin. Then when the sinner has repented of sin and accepted Jesus as Saviour, he is baptized by the Spirit into the body of Christ on earth, the Church. "For by one Spirit are we all baptized into one body... and have been all made to drink into one Spirit" (I Cor. 12:13). This then becomes the first event in the life of the Christian. The Holy Spirit is the baptizer, the Church is the element into which He baptizes, and the unregenerated sinner is the object that is baptized. Unless this event becomes a new way of life, it has little meaning. "Therefore if any man be in Christ, he is a new creature [by the event of regeneration]: old things are passed away; behold, all things are become new" (II Cor. 5:17).

Since the Holy Spirit has baptized this new member into the body, it becomes the duty of the body (the Church) to recognize this act of the Spirit by baptizing the new believer in water. The Church is the agent, water is the element, and the new Christian is the object. This then becomes the second event in his life. He has now received the Spirit (Ezek. 36:26; John 1:12, 13; John 3:6–8) and has been accepted into the Church. There remains one more step or event. The regenerated sinner, now a member of the Christian Church, must be baptized in the Holy Spirit by the Lord Jesus Christ, the head of the Church. Christ is the agent, the Holy Spirit is the element, and the believer is the object.

An Encounter with Christ

Being baptized by the Spirit into the body is not an encounter with the Church but with the Holy Spirit. Baptism in water is not an encounter with the water but with the Church. The baptism into the Holy Spirit is not an encounter with the Spirit but with Christ, the baptizer. This means total surrender and absolute commitment to Jesus. Without this He cannot baptize you in the Spirit.

The image that John the Baptist gave of this ministry of Christ is one of total immersion into the river. The candidate does not receive the river (he did that when he drank from the river. John 4: 14, I Cor. 12: 13). It is now the river receiving or overflowing the candidate (John 7: 38, 39). The candidate who came to Jordan for baptism did not splash around in the water. He did not swim in the river. He took no deep dive to get baptized. Quietly, determinedly, reverently, he walked into the river till he stood close by the baptizer. At that point he stopped all his action and fully surrendered to the baptizer. In a moment, indeed in a few seconds, the baptism is complete. Then again the candidate begins to act by returning to the bank.

Anyone who has accepted Christ as Saviour and has been regenerated by the Spirit can enter into this relationship with Christ. Even in complete solitude one may very quietly and reverently sit back as they did on the day of Pentecost (they were sitting) and in the house of Cornelius (they sat listening to Peter) and let Jesus do it all. You cannot pray or praise yourself into this experience. You surrender to Christ and He gives you the experience. But keep your mind on Christ (II Cor. 10: 5, 6) while you wait for the experience. As sure as one feels the effect of the water upon the body, so may you feel the effect of the Holy Spirit within your body. At that moment you know the Spirit has taken over. You may tremble or shake or feel some deep stir within, but from the record of Scripture there is only one thing that you can expect. It happened every time according to Acts 2: 4, 10: 44–46, 19: 6.

Speak with Tongues and Magnify God

"He that speaketh in an unknown tongue speaketh not
unto men, but unto God: for no man understandeth him; howbeit
in the spirit he speaketh mysteries" (I Cor. 14:2). That makes
sense. You speak to God and He understands. That is all that
matters, for this is the moment of total surrender to Him. This
is absolute commitment, and He takes the helm to set your ship
on a new course (James 3:2, 4, 5). Then you discover the
truth of Paul's testimony: "He that speaketh in an unknown
tongue edifieth himself" (I Cor. 14:4). This is the beginning
of a new life of ministry. As soon as you are edified you will
want to edify others. Then there follow the other manifestations
of the Spirit according to I Corinthians 12:7.

Who Speaks, the Spirit or You?

BOTH! You speak as He gives utterance. You talk to God
with words that He gives upon your lips. You will find the
principle is the same as in Mark 13:11: "It is not ye that speak,
but the Holy Ghost." Furthermore, this is an act of faith on
your part: "These signs shall follow them that *believe*...they
shall speak with new tongues" (Mark 16:17). The moment you
believe His word, His promises, you dare to speak, and the
Spirit gives utterance. The moment you doubt, it stops, and for
those who only doubt and never believe, this manifestation of
the Spirit never begins.

Christians who have never heard the kind of doctrine that
says: "This is not for our day, this may be evil, and this is
sheer emotion," do not find it difficult to co-operate with the Spirit
and to speak as He gives utterance. But those who have learned
and preached this corrupt doctrine about the manifestations
and gifts of the Holy Spirit find tremendous mental blocks in
their subconscious mind. Often they suffer under a severe guilt-
complex and have to believe *first* that "he is faithful and just
to forgive us" (I John 1:9). The moment you accept remission
of sins (Acts 10:43), the language of the Spirit will flow from
your lips. You will then discover the truth of II Timothy 1:7.
You have received the Spirit of "power, and of love, and of a

sound mind." The love will stir your deepest and most sacred emotions. Tears may trickle over your cheeks, but He also has a sound mind, and you will not act crazy, but will glorify God with new tongues, unknown to you, yet understood by Him.

I have enjoyed this form of devotion for forty-five years. Every word written by Paul and others has been confirmed by my experience. I have no need to speculate on the meaning of the Word, for the Word has been made "flesh" in my own life as a member of the body of Christ. In the beginning I had the wilderness experience and the enemy challenged everything that I had, but I never depended on my experience. I always sought to be sure "it is written," just as Jesus did. Now I can easily and regularly follow the advice of the Apostle Paul: "Stir up the *gift of God*, which is in thee" (II Tim. 1:6). I can stir Him up any time, anywhere, and I have found "the Spirit also helpeth our infirmities: for we know not what we should pray for as we ought; but the Spirit himself maketh intercession for us with groanings [to the mind that is what tongues sound like] which cannot be uttered [with the mind]" (Rom. 8:26).

PRAYING WITH THE SPIRIT

"They that wait upon the Lord shall renew [change] their strength" (Isa. 40:31). "Wait for the promise of the Father... and ye shall be baptized [changed] with the Holy Ghost" (Acts 1:4, 5).

"The Spirit also helpeth our infirmities: for we know not what we should pray for as we ought: but the Spirit itself maketh intercession for us with groanings which cannot be uttered" (Rom. 8:26).

"He that speaketh [prayeth] in an unknown tongue speaketh [prayeth] not unto men, but unto God: for no man understandeth him; howbeit in the spirit he speaketh [prayeth] mysteries" (I Cor. 14:2).

"For if I pray in an unknown tongue, *my spirit prayeth*, but my understanding is unfruitful. What is it then? I will pray with the spirit, and I will pray with the understanding also: I will sing with the spirit, and I will sing with the understanding also" (I Cor. 14:14, 15).

"I would that ye *all spake* [or prayed] with tongues, but rather that ye prophesied [or spoke with the understanding]:...that the church may receive edifying" (I Cor. 14:5).

"He that speaketh [or prayeth] in an unknown tongue *edifieth himself*; but he that prophesieth edifieth the church" (I Cor. 14:4).

"Forasmuch as ye are zealous of spiritual gifts [manifestations], seek that ye may excel to the edifying of the church" (I Cor. 14:12).

"In the church I had rather speak five words with my understanding, that...I might teach others also [edify the church], than ten thousand words in an unknown tongue" (I Cor. 14:19).

But at home, in private devotions, he says: "I thank my God, I speak [pray] with tongues *more than ye all*" (I Cor. 14:18). Yes, even ten thousand words.

How can anyone edify the Church unless he himself is edified? It is clear that Paul knew the secret of "edifying himself" by praying in tongues. That is why he could edify the Church by revelation, by knowledge, by prophesying and by doctrine (I Cor. 14:6). He says: "Even while I prayed in the temple, I was in a trance" (Acts 22:17). That is truly praying in the Spirit. Peter, the great Church builder, also prayed in the Spirit. "Peter went up upon the housetop to pray about the sixth hour [noon]" (Acts 10:9). "I was...praying: and in a trance I saw a vision" (Acts 11:5). *That* was the beginning of the Gentile Church. That was the first step toward Christian missions. It was praying in the Spirit that brought Peter to obedience to the great commission: "Go ye therefore, and teach all nations" (Matt. 28:19). Until he prayed in the Spirit on the housetop in Joppa he had preached the Gospel "to none but unto the Jews only" (Acts 11:19).

A Serious Question

Lately, more often than formerly, I have been asked the question: What is the need for, the advantage of, or the blessing in speaking or praying with tongues?

From the above Scriptures it must now be clear to you that the great need to pray and sing and worship in the Spirit is taken care of when you speak, sing or pray with tongues. *That is truly praying in the Spirit.*

"The hour cometh, and now is, when the true worshippers shall worship the Father in spirit and in truth: for the Father seeketh such to worship him. God is a Spirit: and they that worship him must worship him in spirit and in truth" (John 4:23, 24).

"Howbeit, when he, the Spirit of truth, is come, he will guide you into all truth: for he shall not speak of himself; but whatsoever he shall hear, that shall he speak: and he will shew you things to come. He shall glorify me: for he shall receive of mine, and shall shew it unto you" (John 16:13, 14).

Do you want to glorify Christ? Do you want to know the mind of Christ? Do you want to know things to come? Then let the Spirit have *His* way and let *Him* pray in you and through you in "unknown tongues," for you always speak and pray with tongues "as the Spirit gives utterance" (Acts 2: 4) .

A Serious Confession

Ministers, missionaries, and others have come to me and said something like this: "I received the baptism in the Holy Spirit long ago. At the time I spoke in tongues just a little, just a sign [I Cor. 1: 22] but never again after that. Now I have no further manifestations of the Spirit. I fear my ministry is cold, even though I claim the baptism in the Spirit. I do not know that overflowing fullness that I believe I should have. Is it because I have not continued to pray with tongues?"

Candidly, I believe it is. You have missed the secret of praying and worshipping in the Spirit. You have prayed "with the understanding" and your intellect has been very active, but your spirit has been starved because you have failed to pray "with the spirit." It is so edifying to pray and to sing "with the spirit" in your private devotions. Yes, even in the church you may pray in tongues in a whisper to God (I Cor. 14: 28) . You have failed to edify yourself, and now you find it impossible to edify the church as you would like to, by "interpretation of tongues," by prophecy and the rest of the manifestations of the Spirit.

"Is it not generally accepted that tongues is the least of all the gifts of the Spirit?" Yes, that may be so. But that is the very reason why you should begin with this manifestation, and the others will follow. Praying with unknown tongues will so edify you that you will soon be able to edify the Church. He first edifies you, then the church through you.

"The Holy Spirit has not given me the 'gift of tongues,' " says another. For the matter of "gifts," let me assure you the Holy Spirit does not give the gift of tongues, or any other gift. He only *manifests* himself through you so that you can give these gifts to the Church for edification (see I Cor. 12: 7) . The manifestation is given to every man, even to you, as He wills (vs. 11) . From the very inception, when you first spoke with tongues as the Spirit gave utterance, it was a manifestation of the Spirit and it always remains just that. Tongues that bring a message by interpretation to the Church is a gift to the Church through the speaker.

A Serious Warning

Are all prophets? (I Cor. 12:29). No, certainly not. But, "Ye may all prophesy one by one, that all may learn, and all may be comforted" (I Cor. 14:31). (See also verse 24—if all prophesy.)

"Do all speak with tongues?" (I Cor. 12:30). No, not in the church. But the Apostle writes: "I would that ye all spake with tongues" (I Cor. 14:5). "I speak with tongues more than ye all" (vs. 18). "If therefore the whole church be come together into one place and all speak with tongues" (vs. 23). All may speak with tongues in private devotions, but only two or three in the church (I Cor. 14:27).

"But covet earnestly the best gifts: and yet show I unto you a more excellent way [than coveting]" (I Cor. 12:31)—not more excellent than gifts. There is no way of edifying the Church but by a manifestation of gifts *through* various members in the body *to* the assembled saints. So the gathered believers should "covet" that the Spirit should manifest the best gifts. "But all these worketh [or manifest] that one and the selfsame Spirit, dividing to every man [not only to apostles, prophets, pastors and teachers] severally *as he will*" (I Cor. 12:11).

"If I speak with the tongues of men and of angels, and have not love, I am become sounding brass, or a clanging cymbal [big noise]" (I Cor. 13:1). Therefore, away with tongues, says someone. Is that so? "If I bestow all my goods to feed the poor... but have not love, it profiteth me nothing" (vs. 3). Therefore, away with benevolent societies and charitable associations? Oh no, that is the very proof of our Christian love. Then why object to tongues?

What if you speak with tongues of men and of angels and have love? Then you become the very oracle of God. But do not covet these blessings for themselves. They are yours if you are Christ's and love Him with all your heart, and all your soul, and all your mind (Matt. 22:37). You must also love your neighbor as yourself (vs. 39). "Hereby perceive we the love of God, because he laid down his life for us: and we ought to lay down our lives for the brethren" (I John 3:16).

"Wherefore, brethren, covet to prophesy [that ye may edify the Church], and *forbid not* to speak with tongues [that the members may edify themselves]" (I Cor. 14:39).

"But, beloved, remember ye the words which were spoken before of the apostles of our Lord Jesus Christ; how that they told you there should be mockers in the last time, who should walk after their own ungodly lusts [speaking great swelling words, having men's persons in admiration because of advantage—Jude 16]. These be they who separate themselves, sensual [or carnal, I Cor. 2:14], having not the Spirit. But ye, beloved, building up yourselves [by praying with tongues, I Cor. 14:4] on your most holy faith, *praying in the Holy Ghost*" (Jude 17–20).

"Praying always with all prayer and supplication in the Spirit [praying in tongues], and watching thereunto with all perseverance and supplication for all saints" (Eph. 6:18). "And he that searcheth the hearts knoweth what is the *mind of the Spirit*, because *he* maketh intercession for the saints, according to the will of God" (Rom. 8:27).

I suggest that *all* ministers, missionaries, and members of all churches seek an encounter with Christ, the mighty Baptizer, for the baptism into the Holy Spirit (Matt. 3:11 and Acts 1:5). Then when you begin to speak with other tongues as the Spirit gives you utterance (Acts 2:4), continue to worship Him in Spirit and in truth, so that you may be edified until your life and ministry are totally dedicated to the edification of the Church. *Cease not to pray with tongues. Forbid not to speak with tongues.*

GLOSSOLALIA

A Testimony

"I am a physicist doing research work for a large chemical company. I am also a seminary graduate and an Episcopal priest."

Thus begins the testimony of the Rev. William O. Swan, published in *Trinity* Magazine, P.O. Box 2422, Van Nuys, California, at Easter of 1962. He continues his story as follows:

"We went into the cathedral for prayers. When I left, I had heard my own lips forming a new language, and I knew they could do it again when I so desired.

"I decided to make speaking in tongues the object of an introspective study. Where does it really come from, in terms of theology, psychology, common sense?... How much imagination is required to make the claims I have heard about?

"To get the answers, I spoke in tongues occasionally throughout the day. I was looking for patterns, repetitive phrases, clues to use for analysis. But the experiment ran into immediate difficulty. That 'before-the-altar' feeling would come upon me within about 45 seconds, and if I persisted for two or three minutes, I would fill with emotion.

"Since then, when I speak in tongues a simple feeling of love will drench my whole person, and appear to leave a permanent stain of love which does not evaporate.

"In three short days the experimental study was over, with practically all my questions still unanswered. I had discovered most powerfully what everyone else seems to assume: *speaking in tongues is prayer!*"

The writer of this article was praying with the Rev. Swan

81

when he received the baptism in the Holy Spirit in St. Paul's Episcopal Cathedral, Detroit, Mich.

Speaking in Tongues Is Prayer

"For one who speaks in an [unknown] tongue speaks not to men *but to God,* for no one understands [him]...because in the [Holy] Spirit he utters secret truths and hidden things [not obvious to the understanding]" (I Cor. 14:2, Amp. N.T.).

"So too the (Holy) Spirit comes to our aid and bears us up in our weakness; for we do not know what prayer to offer nor how to offer it worthily as we ought, but the Spirit Himself goes to meet our supplication and pleads in our behalf with unspeakable yearnings and groanings too deep for utterance. [Writer's note: This I believe is just another way of describing praying in tongues.] And He Who searches the hearts of men knows what is in the mind of the (Holy) Spirit...because the Spirit intercedes and pleads [before God] in behalf of the saints according to and in harmony with God's will" (Rom. 8:26, 27, Amp. N.T.).

The Apostle Paul, who spoke with tongues more than all his contemporaries (I Cor. 1:18), never makes mention of an instance where it would seem that the church or anyone received a message in tongues, or even in tongues and interpretation. He writes: "For if I *pray* in an unknown tongue, my spirit prayeth, but my understanding is unfruitful" (I Cor. 14:14). Then he says: "I will pray with the spirit, and I will pray with the understanding also" (I Cor. 14:15). In verse 16 he says: "Else when thou shalt bless with the spirit [in tongues], how shall he that occupieth the room of the unlearned say Amen at thy giving of thanks [prayer], seeing he understandeth not what thou sayest [in tongues]?"

It seems quite clear to me that Paul considered all speaking in tongues as prayer and as always addressed to God, never a "message" to men.

Prayer can be giving thanks, making intercession, praise, worship, adoration, and confessing our love, admiration, gratitude, and devotion to God. In this we are too often weak, but "the Spirit helpeth our infirmities."

Interpretation of Tongues

Now then, if speaking in tongues is speaking to God, it is always prayer, and the interpretation will always be in the form of prayer—man speaking to God, and not God speaking to men.

Even on the day of Pentecost, when unbelievers heard their own languages spoken by those who were speaking in tongues for the first time, they did not hear messages or sermons addressed to them, but they heard them "speak in...tongues, the wonderful works of God."

Then also in the house of Cornelius: "They heard them talking in [unknown] languages and extolling and magnifying God" (Acts 10:46, Amp. N.T.).

Paul says: "I would that ye all spake with tongues, but rather that ye prophesied: for greater is he that prophesieth than he that speaketh in tongues, except he interpret, that the church may receive edifying" (I Cor. 14:5). Thus, tongues followed by interpretation edifies the Church, and so also "he that prophesieth edifieth the church" (I Cor. 14:4).

Prophecy is edifying to the Church, and tongues plus interpretation edifies the Church. Indeed, both are edifying, but it does not say that tongues plus interpretation is prophecy.

Interpretation must be prayer, for speaking in tongues is speaking to God, and prophesying is speaking "to men for their upbuilding and constructive spiritual progress and encouragement and consolation" (I Cor. 14:3, Amp. N.T.).

All too often we hear of a "message in tongues." There is no such term, or suggestion in the New Testament. It should rather be "a prayer in tongues" or perhaps "an utterance in tongues."

"He that speaketh in an unknown tongue edifieth himself" (vs. 4). Naturally, because speaking to God in prayer, no matter where or when or how, will always edify, comfort or encourage the one who prays. The more edified anyone is the more hope there is of being used of the Spirit to edify others in the Church.

Since speaking in tongues is prayer, it does not mean that what follows "an utterance in tongues" must be interpretation. It could very well be an answer to the prayer just uttered by the

Spirit, for prayer, real prayer, should be a dialogue between Father and child, and our Father speaks to His children in prophecy.

Some Questions on Interpretation

I have prayed with multitudes who came to seek the baptism in the Holy Spirit from the mighty Baptizer, the Lord Jesus Christ. He said: "Those who believe... will speak in new languages" (Mark 16:17, Amp. N.T.).

Even after forty years of experience I never cease to thrill when I pray with those who encounter Christ as their Baptizer (John 1:33, 34) and hear them begin to speak "new tongues," "other tongues," "unknown tongues," or "divers kinds of tongues," as the Spirit gives utterance. Yes indeed, they speak but it is the Spirit who gives utterance. He forms the words on their lips as they speak by faith in Him, to magnify God.

Then someone will ask: "While I was speaking in tongues it seemed I received a strange understanding of what I was saying to God in tongues. Was that interpretation?" Yes, the Holy Spirit quickened your understanding to know what He was saying to God in an unknown tongue through your tongue.

Someone else asks: "As I was speaking in tongues it seemed as if I received through my understanding some new revelations and some answers to my problems. Was that interpretation?" No, that was not interpretation. That was answer to your prayer. That was the dialogue between you and the Father. You speak to Him in tongues and He speaks to you through your understanding. Any revelation that comes to you personally through your understanding is never interpretation, for speaking in tongue is speaking to God. The Father does not speak to you in tongues, you speak to Him in tongues.

Then again comes another question: "While I was speaking in tongues, I received a message for the Church (or for someone) was that interpretation?" No, that was not interpretation. That was prophecy, and you should learn to speak out such revelations, very calmly, reverently, and confidently. It may be the answer to the prayer in the Spirit that you have prayed for others, or for the Church. Do not get excited and shout or scream out the words.

Lately I have often been asked: "How can I know what is interpretation and what is prophecy?" Interpretation of tongues is always addressed to God and ends in Him. Prophecy is addressed to the people, for edification, exhortation, and comfort.

Some Common Misunderstandings

Recently a minister said to me: "I have some real problems in regard to interpretation of tongues in my church. Someone will speak in a tongue and it sounds like a prayer repeated two or three times. Then another will begin to interpret, but there is no repetition in the interpretation. In fact the interpretation usually lasts much longer than the tongues. Those who listen carefully feel that they cannot accept this as true interpretation."

I think they are right. Why should everything that follows an utterance in tongues necessarily be interpretation? Suppose you heard someone pray in your own language: "Lord, bless Thy people; they need edification. O Lord, Thy people need exhortation today. Dear Lord, speak a word of comfort to Thy people." Would you be surprised if this prayer is followed by a rather lengthy word of prophecy that is truly edifying and comforting? No, not at all. Then why not accept for your guidance the Scriptural principle that speaking in tongues is prayer and what follows may often be the answer to the prayer and not the interpretation of the prayer.

Then my friend asked further: "How is it that sometimes a person will commence to speak with tongues, just a few sentences, and then he proceeds to interpret himself, but he gives a long message and does not revert back to tongues again. Was that interpretation?" No, that was prayer in tongues, followed by prophecy.

Prayer can lead to the most wonderful answers and experiences. No matter who speaks in tongues, or how long or short the utterance, I always accept it all as prayer. If the speaker in tongues or someone else follows with words like: "O Lord our God, how great Thou art," and then continues in that strain, speaking to God, I know that is pure interpretation.

May We Speak With Tongues Any Time?

Surely, we can pray any time and anywhere. So why not pray in tongues any time? The Holy Spirit has become resident within us and He is there twenty-four hours a day, every day, all the year round. Paul writes to Timothy: "Wherefore I put thee in remembrance that thou stir up the gift of God, which is in thee by the putting on of my hands." (Writer's note: I believe Paul prayed for Timothy when he received the baptism in the Holy Spirit, just like he prayed for the Ephesians in Acts 19:6.)

Paul further reminds Timothy: "For God hath not given us the spirit of fear; but of power, and of love, and of a sound mind" (II Tim. 1:6, 7). How we need this power, this love and a sound mind. Stir Him up and pray in His power, His love, and His sound mind, at all times and anywhere.

I do not think anyone has ever fathomed the depth and the grace that comes from praying with the Spirit. No wonder Paul thanked God that he prayed with tongues more than all. Look at the grace, the wisdom, the power, and the ministry that Paul enjoyed on earth. He found it wise to speak but five words with the understanding in the church, after he had prayed ten thousand words in a tongue at home.

Then comes the question: "Why can we speak in tongues any time and yet we cannot interpret or prophesy any time?" Because speaking in tongues is speaking to God and it edifies the speaker, but interpretation and prophecy are speaking to men; therefore men should be present to hear in order to receive edification. The "speaker in tongues" always needs edification and can receive it anywhere, any time, by praying in tongues. However, let all our speaking or praying in tongues always be very reverent, for we are speaking to our heavenly Father.

Is Speaking in Tongues a Gift?

The ability to speak with tongues is not a gift. It is a "manifestation of the Spirit" (I Cor. 12:7).

New tongues, Mark 16:17; other tongues, Acts 2:4; tongues, Acts 10:46 and 19:6; diversities of tongues, I Cor. 12:10, 28; unknown tongues, I Cor. 14:2, 4, 5, 6, 13, 14, 18, 22, 26, 27, and 39.

are ALL simply manifestations of the Spirit (I Cor. 12:7), and are spoken by believers (Mark 16:17), with the Spirit (I Cor. 14:14, 15), which means "yielding to" or "co-operating with" the Holy Spirit. The term "gift of tongues" was coined by those who did not have the experience.

All gifts of the Spirit (I Cor. 12:4) are actually and simply manifestations of the Spirit (I Cor. 12:7), and they are not enablements in the sense that anyone may possess the *ability* to "use the gift."

To write this article I am using a typewriter. This machine can write letters, words, and sentences, but never unless someone uses it. Of itself it can do nothing, but I can cause it to write what I want. The Holy Spirit causes us to do what He wants, if only we will be as cooperative as the typewriter.

Even Jesus never claimed any ability as a gift He possessed. He says: "I assure you . . . the Son is able to do nothing from Himself—of His own accord; but He is able to do only what He sees the Father doing" (John 5:19, Amp. N.T.).

He teaches His disciples that when they meet any challenge in councils or courts, they should "say whatever is given you in that hour and at that moment, for it is not you who will be speaking but the Holy Spirit" (Mark 13:11, Amp. N.T.). This is the principle or basis on which the Holy Spirit manifests His gifts through believers.

Personally I have learned not to claim to possess any gift of the Spirit, but I do possess *the Gift of God* (and He possesses me) which is the Spirit of power, and of love, and of a sound mind. He will manifest himself through me, or anyone else, as He will (I Cor. 12:11).

Like Paul the Apostle, I have discovered that the Holy Spirit who seeks to build up the Church will always most certainly first build up or edify the one He uses to edify the Church. I have learned to pray with tongues any time, anywhere, to receive assurance, power, and wisdom or whatever is needed for my edification. In such cases the ability to speak with tongues is not the gift I have, but rather the effect of praying with tongues is the gift of the Spirit to me.

I consider that any manifestation of the Spirit that may come through me, such as the word of wisdom, word of knowledge, prophecy, healing, and so forth, are gifts of the Spirit to my listeners—not to me, but through me to the others.

When Are Tongues a Sign?

Jesus said: "These *signs* shall follow them that believe... they shall speak with new tongues" (Mark 16:17).

Paul says: "Wherefore tongues are for a *sign*, not to them that believe, but to them that believe not" (I Cor. 14:22).

On the day of Pentecost the believers "were filled with the Holy Ghost, and began to speak with other tongues, as the Spirit gave them utterance" (Acts 2:4). The unbelievers, out of every nation under heaven, "were confounded, because that every man heard them speak his own language...the wonderful works of God" (Acts 2:6 and 11). This surely was a sign to those that believed not, that God was in them of a truth (I Cor. 14:25).

During the past forty years I know of many instances where total unbelievers and severe critics heard someone speak in what to the speaker was an "unknown" tongue, but to the listener it was his own mother-tongue. In such cases it may be unknown tongues to the one who speaks, but it sounds like prophecy to the one who understands that language. I think this is where we get confused with Paul's statement in I Corinthians 14:22–25.

It seems that he speaks of tongues as being prophecy, understandable to the unbeliever, and yet not understandable to the speaker. Only when one has witnessed such cases can one really grasp the meaning of "tongues are for a sign."

It is a great pity that many have interpreted tongues to be *a sign of the baptism in the Holy Spirit*, and so they are satisfied with speaking just a few words in tongues.

People in Pentecostal movements are very fond of the expression, "Tongues is the *initial* evidence of the baptism in the Holy Spirit." This is not found in Scripture, but it is nevertheless the truth according to the record in the Acts, from the day of Pentecost onward.

No other sign could have given greater assurance, for they had cast out devils, healed the sick, done miracles, spoken the word of wisdom and of knowledge, and prophesied *before* the day of Pentecost. All the manifestations of the Holy Spirit are found in the Old Testament, except speaking with tongues.

In the case of Samaria (Acts 8:8–17) there is no mention of tongues. But how did they know that they had not received the Holy Ghost (vs. 16), and how did they know that they did when they had laid hands upon them? (vs. 17). How did Simon recognize that anything had happened to them? (vs. 18).

Well, how did they know that they had received in the house of Cornelius? (Acts 10:44–46). There was no time to see whether they could heal the sick or do miracles or prophesy, but they knew at once, "for they heard them speak with tongues, and magnify God" (vs. 46). By the same token Paul knew when he prayed for the Ephesians. "They spake with tongues, and prophesied" (Acts 19:6).

However, let us remember that tongues is more than a sign, more than an initial evidence, more than a strange phenomenon. To pray with the Spirit in tongues is the most edifying experience that any child of God can have. The practice of praying in tongues should continue and increase in the lives of those who are baptized in the Spirit, otherwise they may find that the other manifestations of the Spirit come seldom or stop altogether. If you wish to edify your brethren in the church, then keep on edifying yourself by the constant practice of praying with the Spirit in your private devotions. Tongues are not for public ministry but for private devotions, at home and in the church.

When to Pray for Interpretation

"So it is with yourselves; since you are so eager. . .to possess . . .manifestations of the (Holy) Spirit, [concentrate on] striving to excel and to abound [in them] in ways which will build up the church. Therefore, the person who speaks in an [unknown] tongue [in the church] should pray [for the power] to interpret" (I Cor. 14:12, 13,.Amp. N.T.).

There is nowhere any suggestion that anyone should pray for "the gift of interpretation." The speaker in tongues is told to pray that he may interpret by the Spirit; then that interpretation becomes the gift of the Spirit to the Church for edification.

I strongly hold to the position that neither the Church nor anyone in the church should ever lay hands on any person that he may receive any gifts of the Spirit, but only that he may receive the gift of God, which is the Holy Spirit. The Apostles never laid hands on anyone to receive gifts of the Spirit.

Paul simply admonishes the Church to "covet earnestly the best gifts" (I Cor. 12:31), and warns them that "forasmuch as ye are zealous of spiritual gifts [writer's note: I prefer the word "manifestations" to that of "gifts" used by the King James translators], seek that ye may excel to the edifying of the church" (I Cor. 14:12). Here the golden rule is, "All for the edifying of the Church."

Now, what are the best gifts? Only the Holy Spirit will know this. He alone will know in every gathering just which of the manifestations will bring the greatest blessing or the most edification to the believers and unbelievers. Whatever is needed most will always be the best. He knows our every need and the will of God.

There is great danger (and no Scripture) to lay hands on those who have just received the baptism in the Spirit and begin to speak with tongues that they might interpret what they say Let them speak to God and not to man, and let them speak mysteries.

The wisest thing we can do is to advise novices in the things of the Spirit to learn to yield to Him that they may soon be used by Him to manifest himself through them, bringing forth any of the "gifts" that may be needed by others. First let the Spirit edify or build them into channels that He can use. Since the most edifying manifestation is prophecy, one should expect that the Spirit will manifest prophetic gifts rather than interpretation.

Regulate but Do Not Forbid Tongues

Now comes the question of how much tongues and interpretation or prophecy there should be in any gathering or in the church.

Paul writes: "If some speak in a [strange] tongue, let the number be limited to two or at the most three, and each one [taking his] turn, and let one interpret and explain....But if ther is no one [writer's note: among the three] to do the interpreting, let each of them keep still in the church and talk to himself and to God" (I Cor. 14: 27, 28, Amp. N.T.). Here is good advice. If you feel moved by the Spirit, then "whisper" in tongues but do not stop speaking.

However, note that the question of interpretation is only imperative when there is a loud and clear speaking in tongues in the church. It seems quite clear that the Apostle did not expect interpretation to follow after the first utterance in tongues. Only after two or three such utterances *must* there be interpretation. Otherwise, it would seem that the Holy Spirit did not deem that interpretation is needed for the edification of that gathering.

I believe that inasmuch as the next verse clearly states that there should be no more than two or three prophets who speak, it is always wise to limit interpretations to two or three in any meeting. From personal experience and observation, I would say that we have far too many interpretations and not nearly enough prophecies in most gatherings. Paul urges that all should seek to prophesy (I Cor. 14: 1).

"Wherefore, brethren, covet to prophesy, and *forbid not* to speak with tongues. Let all things be done decently and in order" (I Cor. 14: 39, 40).

Note: Those texts followed by (Amp. N.T.) are quoted from the Amplified New Testament. All others are from the King James Version.

(The foregoing may be obtained in free tract form from the writer.)

GIFTS OR MANIFESTATIONS
OF THE SPIRIT

"Brethren, I would not have you ignorant" (I Cor. 12:1).

In church services there is nothing more distressing than the shocking ignorance about, and the lamentable absence of, the gifts of the Holy Spirit. Even in our Pentecostal churches, where there is evidence of more liberty in the Spirit, we find far more physical and emotional reaction to the presence of the Spirit than true manifestations of the gifts of the Spirit. Ignorance causes many to fail to recognize real manifestations of the word of wisdom and the word of knowledge by attributing these to the intellect of the speakers. While there are fewer manifestations of the gifts than we *claim*, there are often more than we *recognize*, because of ignorance.

Let me say right here that I consider it heresy to speak of shaking, trembling, falling, dancing, clapping, shouting, and such actions as manifestations of the Holy Spirit. These are purely human reactions to the power of the Holy Spirit and frequently hinder more than help to bring forth genuine manifestations. There are far too many Christians who are satisfied with such emotional reactions and thus do not seek to grow in grace and become channels through whom the Holy Spirit may manifest His gifts for the edification of the Church. If we remember the admonition of Paul, "Let all things be done unto edifying" (I Cor. 14:26), there are many things that we shall stress and encourage far less than we do now. There is a need, and good reason, for babies to cry, but they must be taught to stop crying and learn to speak (I Cor. 13:11). I recognize the need for bright and happy song services (I Cor. 14:15), but there must be a time and place for the ministry of the Word and the manifestation of the Spirit (I Cor. 14:26).

Do I hear some pastor say: "But how do we get the gifts of the Spirit? Why do not those who have the gifts operate them?

The operation of the gifts often causes embarrassing situations in the service. We do not understand how to regulate the operation of the gifts in the Church." Yes, I have often heard such utterances.

Let us get it clear. Spiritual gifts are not operated; they are manifested by the Spirit. Such gifts are not perpetual enablements. They are miraculous, supernatural, and instantaneous manifestations of the Holy Spirit. No man can use the gifts of the Spirit, but the Spirit can use any man to manifest any gift as He wills (I Cor. 12:11).

Translators of the King James Version have caused great confusion by inserting the word *gifts* in I Cor. 12:1; I Cor. 13:2; I Cor. 14:1; and I Cor. 14:12. If we substitute the word *manifestations* for gifts in these verses, the meaning is clear and comes into line with the key to the whole problem in verse 7 of I Corinthians 12: "But the manifestation of the Spirit is given to every man to profit withal." "For to one is given by the Spirit [the manifestation of, not the gift of] the word of wisdom [not wisdom]; to another [the manifestation of] the word of knowledge [not knowledge] by the same Spirit; to another [the manifestation of] faith by the same Spirit; to another [the manifestation of] the gifts of healing [the sick receive the gifts of healing] by the same Spirit; to another [the manifestation of] the working of miracles; to another [the manifestation of] prophecy; to another [the manifestation of] discerning of spirits; to another [the manifestation of] divers kinds of tongues; to another [the manifestation of] the interpretation of tongues. But all these worketh [or manifests] that one and the selfsame Spirit, dividing to every man severally *as he will*" (I Cor. 12:8–11) .

Thus, every one of the nine gifts of the Spirit is a manifestation—instantaneous, miraculous, and supernatural—of the Spirit himself. Then why are they called gifts? Because they are given to the Church for profit (I Cor. 12:7) or edification (I Cor. 14:12). The word of wisdom comes as a manifestation of the Spirit in a member and is then a gift to the Church. Prophecy is first a manifestation of the Spirit through a member and then a gift of the Spirit to the Church. Remember, the 11th, 12th, 13th, and 14th chapters of I Corinthians are written to give directions for the *conduct* of those who "come together in the church" (I Cor. 11:

18, 20, 33; I Cor. 14: 19, 23, 26). Therefore, the Apostle admonishes the Corinthians to allow the Spirit to manifest himself through man as He will. "There are diversities of gifts [nine of them], but the same Spirit" (I Cor. 12:4). "There are differences of administrations [Eph. 4:11 and I Cor. 12:28–30], but the same Lord" (I Cor. 12:5). "There are diversities of operations [salvation, healing, prayer, or teaching meetings], but it is the same God which worketh all [these operations] in all [people present]" (I Cor. 12:6). Then comes the great "but." No matter whether the Spirit has many gifts to give, or whether there be present all the different ministries, or what kind of operation in the kingdom of God it may be, the manifestation of the Spirit in such a gathering is given to every man in the meeting, regardless of all these differences.

I submit, then, that anyone who is baptized in the Holy Spirit is a temple of the Spirit, and the Spirit may manifest himself as He will in the nine diverse ways. The gifts are resident in the Spirit and are always manifested by the Spirit himself through the channel in whom the Spirit dwells. We can deliver only what He gives. We can deliver His gifts but we cannot use His gifts.

Then why do we call a man a prophet? Because he has a ministry of prophecy but never a gift to prophesy. There are no "gifts" *to prophesy* or *to heal*. They are gifts of healing, which the sick receive—*not* the evangelist or pastor. For example, we call a fellow a milkman, but all he does is deliver milk. He gets it from the dairy and delivers it to those who have ordered. Actually he has no more to do with the milk than to deliver it. So the healer delivers to the sick what the Holy Spirit gives. The prophet delivers to the Church what the Holy Spirit gives. The teacher delivers to the Church what the Holy Spirit gives. These ministries are the gifts of Christ, the Head of the Church (see Eph. 4:7–12). These ministries are set by God in the Church (see I Cor. 12:28–30). Therefore I hold that when the Apostle says "covet earnestly the best gifts," he means ministry gifts, not gifts of the Spirit.

Yet a more excellent way (than coveting the best ministry gifts) for the manifestation of the Spirit (vs. 31) is chapter 13—LOVE. I may have manifestations of the Spirit and still lack love (the Lord once spoke through a donkey), so in spite of what the Spirit may manifest through me, I am just a big noise, or just nothing, if I have not love. But if I have love *and the manifestation of the Spirit,* I become the oracle of God, even though I may not be an apostle, or prophet, or pastor, or minister of any kind. The Holy Spirit does not manifest gifts to glorify the channel, but to glorify God and to edify the Church.

Now let us take note of a few Scriptures that will clear up the matter still more. Paul writes to Timothy: "Neglect not the gift that is in thee, which was given thee by prophecy, with the laying on of the hands of the presbytery" (I Tim. 4:14). Why do the presbytery lay hands on a man? To ordain him into the ministry. So when they laid hands on Timothy, the Holy Spirit spake by prophecy as in Acts 13:2–4, and the young man became an evangelist (II Tim. 4:5). The context of verse 14 in I Timothy 4 also indicates that it all had to do with the ministry. So Paul simply told Timothy not to neglect the ministry that had been given him by God through prophecy. Then in his second epistle to Timothy, chapter 1, verses 6 and 7, Paul writes: "Wherefore I put thee in remembrance that thou stir up the gift of God, which is in thee by the putting on of my hands. For God hath not given us the spirit of fear; but of power, and of love, and of a sound mind." Here he speaks of the gifts of God, and the Holy Spirit himself *is* the gift of God. Timothy must have received his baptism when Paul laid hands on him, as he did to the Ephesians in Acts 19:6. No stretch of imagination could bring the above two references to "gift" within the meaning of the gifts of the Spirit.

Note carefully in Ephesians 4:7–12, the gifts of Christ are ministries and in Romans 12:4, the Apostle points out that "all members have not the same office [or ministry]." Then in the following verses he mentions ministries and not gifts of the Spirit (I Cor. 1:6, 7): "Even as the testimony of Christ was confirmed in you: so that ye come behind in no gift." The Church at Corinth did not lack any ministry gift. In I Corinthians 12:28 the Apostle speaks no longer of the gifts or manifestations of the Spirit, but he shows that there are certain ministries in the Church. In the present-day Pentecostal Movement we know that there are those who have an apostolic ministry (missionaries we call them now); others have a prophetic ministry; still others have a teaching ministry; some have a healing ministry (but never the gift to heal), and they impart gifts of healing to the sick as the Holy Spirit manifests himself through them. Then there are those who have a ministry of miracles. Others seem to have a tongues ministry, but this is not a gift to speak in tongues. They just speak to the Church in tongues more often than some. Then again there are those who have an interpretation ministry, but not the gift to interpret. They only interpret tongues more frequently than others.

Ministries are *set* (I Cor. 12:28) and continue "for the perfecting of the saints, for the work of the ministry" (Eph. 4:12). Peter admonishes us to be "good stewards" (I Pet. 4:10, 11) and to minister with the "ability which God giveth." The milkman does not make milk; he delivers it. The telegraph boy does not draft the telegrams; he delivers what he receives. The mailman does not write the letters; he delivers what he receives. Just so in our ministries we do not make or create, but we deliver what the Holy Spirit gives or creates.

Gifts of the Spirit are not set; they are manifested—supernaturally, instantly, and miraculously. Every manifestation is a gift to the Church or someone in the Church. All gifts edify the Church. But there is one that edifies the speaker: "He that speaketh in an unknown tongue *edifieth himself*" (I Cor. 14:4). It would be a great blessing if every Spirit-filled Christian would edify himself before he comes to the service in the church by "praying with the spirit" (I Cor. 14:15) at home. After St. Paul had done his "speaking ten thousand words [vs. 19] with tongues ['more than ye all,' verse 18]," he found that five words with the understanding was dynamite in the church. I truly believe that because there is so little of this "edifying oneself" at home, there is so little of the manifestation of the Spirit to edify the Church. Far too many have the habit of edifying themselves in the church, and this the Apostle discourages in chapter 14, verse 23. But "praying with the Spirit" is permitted, except when you are asked to lead in prayer (vss. 14 to 16). Let us also remember verse 39: "Forbid *not* to speak with tongues."

I often hear it said: "But tongues is the least of all the gifts." My answer is: "Then that is the best reason why all should begin with tongues." If you will begin with tongues and edify yourself, you will soon be interpreting tongues and edifying the Church.

After that you will be prophesying and edifying the Church even more. Now, dear reader, do you see how you may come to have manifestations of the Spirit without praying and fasting for gifts? They all come just like tongues as the Spirit gives utterance. When you have learned to yield to the Spirit to speak with tongues, then you know the secret of how to yield to Him to speak interpretation and to prophesy or even to give the word of wisdom and the word of knowledge. Speaking with tongues, and all that follows, must be by the Spirit.

"Stir up the gift of God which is in thee" (II Tim. 1:6) by being "zealous of spiritual [manifestations]...that ye may excel to the edifying of the church" (I Cor. 14:12). Love sinners and love the saints in the church and you will be most anxious to bless them and bring to them gifts of the Spirit by the manifestation of the Spirit in your life. Those who desire spiritual manifestations in order to show off their deep spirituality get nothing. Even if they do, it sounds mechanical (I Cor. 13:1). But those who "follow after *love*" (I Cor. 14:1) will want to speak "unto men to edification, and exhortation, and comfort" (I Cor. 14:3).

I suggest that we correct our spiritual vocabulary and always speak of the manifestation of the Spirit rather than the gifts of the Spirit. Then when anyone is used of God, let us not say, "He has this or that gift," but recognize the ministry that Christ has given him. Let us stop praying for, striving for, and desiring the "gifts of the Holy Spirit" that we may use them or exercise them. Rather, let us learn how to "yield ourselves unto God" (Rom. 6:13 and 19) that the Holy Spirit may freely manifest His gifts to others through us.

"Let all things be done decently and in order" (I Cor. 14:40).

GATHER THE WHEAT — BURN
THE CHAFF

This message was preached at the opening of the First World Pentecostal Conference in Zurich, Switzerland, in 1947, and subsequently in many churches, Bible schools, and conventions in Europe and North America.

In the beginning of this century when the Holy Spirit was being poured upon holiness groups almost simultaneously everywhere in the world, the first reaction from the established churches was a strong objection to the noise and seeming disorder in the prayer meetings. This was so entirely different from the quiet, almost over-regulated, church services that many religious leaders declared the revival was a wildfire movement. The Pentecostal preachers on the other hand declared boldly that they had received a baptism of the Holy Ghost and fire.

Now, after fifty years, this phenomenal revival has spread to all nations in all countries of the world, and Pentecostal churches have been established. It is nothing unusual, in these days, to hear preachers declare from Pentecostal platforms that many manifestations in some meetings are due to fanaticism if not wildfire. In the beginning we were very fond of considering enthusiastic young converts just filled with the Holy Spirit and full of shout and song as being "on fire." Such on-fire-believers of today look upon the older and experienced Pentecostals as having become lukewarm and cold because they do not demonstrate reactions such as they had when they first came into the Pentecostal experience.

Was the exuberance of the new convert wrong? Has the experienced believer cooled off or backslidden during recent years? Let us look into these questions. First let us study the the grass roots of what is known as the Pentecostal experience.

Just before the birth of Christ, the people sat in darkness. For generations there had been no prophet. There remained only a ceremonial religion. Malachi, the last of the prophets, had said: "Behold, I will send my messenger, and he shall prepare the way before me: and the Lord, whom ye seek, shall suddenly come to his temple, even the messenger of the covenant, whom ye delight in: behold, he shall come, saith the Lord of hosts. But who may abide the day of his coming? and who shall stand when he appeareth? for he is like a refiner's fire, and like fullers' sope: and he shall sit as a refiner and purifier of silver" (Mal. 3:1–3).

The land of Judea is stirred once again. A prophet appears on the scene. He ignores the temple and the synagogues and preaches on the banks of Jordan. He calls everyone to repentance and pronounces judgment upon the self-righteous. To the latter he says: "Think not to say within yourselves, We have Abraham to our father: for I say unto you, that God is able of these stones to raise up children unto Abraham. And now also the ax is laid unto the root of the trees: therefore, every tree which bringeth not forth good fruit is hewn down, and cast into the fire" (Matt. 3:9, 10). Note here—the "fire of judgment."

Suddenly the great prophet turns to the repentant sinners and says: "I indeed baptize you with water unto repentance: but he that cometh after me is mightier than I, whose shoes I am not worthy to bear: he shall baptize you with the Holy Ghost, and with fire [note this is not 'judgment fire' but rather the 'refiner's fire]: whose fan is in his hand, and he will throughly purge his floor, and gather his wheat into the garner; but he will burn up the chaff with unquenchable fire" (Matt. 3:11, 12).

From the words of the prophet it seems clear that a baptism of fire would be needed to burn up the chaff when the wheat had been separated from it. The fan is in the hand of the Baptizer. He will purge His floor; He will burn up the chaff. It is also clear that both the Baptizer and the baptism in the Holy Ghost would be as real as was John and his baptism in water. He declares that the kingdom of heaven is at hand and then tells of the mighty King and the glorious blessings to be expected from His hand.

When Jesus came upon the scene He said: "I will pray the Father, and he shall give you another Comforter, that he may abide with you for ever. . . . But the Comforter, which is the

Holy Ghost, whom the Father will send in my name, he shall teach you all things...he shall testify of me" (John 14:16, 26; 15:26). In confirming the prophecy of John about the coming of the Holy Ghost, the Lord Jesus emphasized the fact that He will be a Comforter. Small wonder then that those who receive the baptism of the Holy Spirit become so exuberant with joy. Such persons are not "on fire" as was often said, but they are "filled with the Holy Ghost." The consequence is that they produce the same manifestations as the first disciples did on the day of Pentecost. It was on that very day that the religious world began to register objections and accuse the Spirit-filled believers of being filled with new wine. It is no different today. We have the same Holy Spirit, the same baptism, the same manifestations—tongues and apparent drunkenness—and the same objections and accusations.

What was Peter's defense? "This is that!" What? The fulfillment of the prophecy of Joel: "In the last days, saith God, I will pour out my Spirit...your sons and your daughters shall prophesy." But the prophet says nothing about speaking in tongues and acting like drunken people. Yes, this is the beginning of that. From now on He will lead into all truth. Prophecy will follow.

Now, pardon a little of my personal testimony. Some years ago I passed through one of those spiritual crises which come into the experience of every growing Christian. I was hungry for a deeper experience with God. I was tired of the repetition of spiritual manifestations which did not seem to bring edification to anyone but myself. I wanted to see the manifestation of the Holy Spirit in operation in my life. One night in desperation I decided I would not go to sleep until the Lord had given me some very definite guidance. My prayer was, "Lord, where must I go from here? This is not the end of the road, for I have always declared that the baptism in the Holy Ghost is only the beginning and not the end of a closer walk with God." After midnight He spoke to me clearly and said that I needed a baptism of fire. Immediately I concluded that because I was no longer as demonstrative as before and did not shout and speak in tongues as loud and long as I did twenty-five years before, I must have lost the fire. I prayed with all my heart that He would baptize me with fire, whatever that might mean. The yielding of that night brought profound things into my life, and my ministry did change. I was a happy man, but I had no desire to shout and sing and leap before the Lord as I did in my younger days. I was ready to do so, but it seemed the Lord did not require that from me.

After enjoying the wonderful deeper life for a few weeks, I discovered that some very cherished things in my life were dropping off. Some of my brethren seemed to misunderstand me. My best friends seemed most unsympathetic. I felt so lonely at times that life became a burden. Again I sought guidance and light from the Lord, for I feared to trust in man.

One Sunday morning, very early, I made my way into a wilderness and lay myself in the dust before the Lord. I felt as if twenty-five years of Christian life and years of ministry were all in vain. Nothing remained and I was just an utter failure. As I wept before the Lord and humbled myself, a peace that passeth understanding suddenly came over my soul. I lay almost as dead. Then it seemed someone was speaking to me in very gentle tones. He said: "I am answering your prayer. It is the baptism of fire." I complained that I did not feel "on fire" at all.

Then He said: "But the fire does not bring joy. It burns, it devours, it reduces, it purges. The Holy Spirit gives comfort and joy, but the fire cleanses and sanctifies. I am removing the chaff from your life." Once again I began to weep and asked the Lord to show me what sin there was still in my life. Very gently I heard Him say: "Chaff is not sin. I am not removing tares but chaff. Chaff is good and indeed it is essential in order to obtain wheat. When the chaff is removed you will see the wheat."

I shall never forget those wonderful moments in His presence. It seemed that He brought me to a green field. I recognized it as growing wheat. Then I found myself in a barn and saw bags of wheat. It seemed as if I were listening to a conversation between two persons. As the one passed his hands through the wheat in the bag he told the other that this was clean rich wheat. We left the barn and looked on the field again. "Beautiful green grass," said the one. "No! Beautiful growing wheat," said the other. "How can that be? This does not look nearly like the things in the bag." "Yet it is true...this is that and that is this. If you will leave this to develop, it will produce wheat such as in the bag, but when you plant what is in the bag, it dies and lives again to produce what you see here."

Again I saw the wheat field. Now it had grown higher and in the gentle breezes the heads of ripening wheat waved to and fro. I heard one say, "Soon it will be ripe and then it must be gathered to the floor where the chaff can be separated from the wheat. The chaff has served its purpose and if it be not removed soon, it will destroy the wheat crop. If, however, you remove the chaff before the wheat is ripe, you will have no crop either. Just one more rain and there will be enough moisture to ripen this wonderful field." I stood amazed. There I saw tall stalks of straw and the ears of wheat were only six inches long. Why, even the wheat kernels were surrounded and covered with chaff. What a process the gathering and threshing is. A threshing floor looks anything but orderly. In the end, however, the winnowing fan separates wheat and chaff and order is restored.

After this revelation I was left alone with my thoughts. What could it all mean? Then I remembered my earliest Pentecostal experience. How often I just wondered whether all the noise and manifestation in a prayer meeting was produced by the power of the Holy Spirit. But why should people want to act so queer and get great blessing out of it? At such times I heard a still small voice say to me, "This is that." I was satisfied, because that was the answer Peter gave on the day of Pentecost. Later on I saw and heard and personally experienced very clear manifestations of the gifts of the Holy Spirit. Instead of tongues only, there followed the interpretation of tongues. Instead of only tongues and interpretation, there followed prophecy. In the sermons of my brethren and in my own messages I began to discern moments when preaching was prophecy, moments when there was the word of wisdom, and moments when there was a word of knowledge.

How did all this come about? Where did it begin? This is how I see it now. First stammering lips, then new tongues, then interpretation of tongues, then prophecy, then words of wisdom and knowledge, all by the same Spirit.

"So is the kingdom of God, as if a man should cast seed into the ground; and should sleep, and rise night and day, and the seed should spring and grow up, he knoweth not how. For the earth bringeth forth fruit of herself; first the blade, then the ear, after that the full corn in the ear. But when the fruit is brought forth, immediately he putteth in the sickle, because the harvest is come" (Mark 4:26–29). Just as the growing wheat on the field responds to every little breeze, so young Christians filled with the Holy Spirit will respond to the breezes of heaven. Just sing a chorus over again and they begin to rejoice and wave their hands. I have noticed that the converts of very sedate and calm preachers are just as emotional as the converts of the shouting and running evangelist. Some of these sedate old preachers were, in fact, very demonstrative in their early Christian experience. The precious brother or sister who now brings such wonderful messages in tongues and interpretation or in prophecy was once as noisy as some of the worst shouters among the young converts. Most mature Christians have found that it took years before they learned to yield to the Holy Ghost so that He might use their lips to prophesy rather than to speak in tongues. Paul thinks that five words that can be understood are worth more than ten thousand words in a tongue that cannot be understood. But then there is usually several feet of chaff before there comes the ear of grain. There might be years of seeming useless manifestations before we ripen into faith that will produce prophecy (Rom. 12:6).

In our Pentecostal churches today, there seem to be two extremes. The Apostle has a word of warning for both. To those who object so fervently against noise and disorder he says: "Quench not the Spirit" (I Thess. 5:19). To those who want nothing but these disorderly manifestations he says: "Despise not prophesyings" (I Thess. 5:20). If you refuse to have seemingly needless manifestations, chaff as you may think, you will never have the gifts of prophecy. If you refuse to let the Lord fan the needless demonstrations from your life and will cling to the initial reactions only, you will never have the ripened fruit of the gifts of the Spirit. The Apostle was quite aware of this, and so he wrote that wonderful chapter 14 in the first epistle to the Corinthians. This chapter will never quench the Spirit, but it will regulate the growth of the saints in the church.

Have you ever watched a modern threshing machine that has taken the place of the old-fashioned threshing floor? There is a lot of shaking and trembling and noise. On the one side there is a mountain of chaff and on the other just a few bags of wheat. What a lot of chaff to produce so little wheat. Put a match in the chaff and what remains will be nothing, compared to the wheat in the bags.

Let us get the correct perspective of spiritual things. Be tolerant and thank God for the growing wheat. Be in no hurry to separate the chaff. Remember the fan is in His hand. On the other hand, we must not be satisfied with a good old shouting camp meeting. Let us honor the Holy Ghost and give Him opportunities to speak to us, for He came not only to comfort us but to lead us into all truth. If we only make noise in our meetings, we shall not hear His voice. Let us have the waving grain when the breezes blow, and thank God for it, but do not judge those who have no part in such demonstration, for not even a hurricane will make a bag of wheat wave. We need wheat for new fields and we need growing fields for more wheat.

There is nothing that can ever take the place of the Holy Spirit in the church. Let us pray for a greater outpouring than ever; and remember when the floods come, it will not keep to our well-prepared channels, but it will overflow and most probably cause chaos in our regular programs.

In recent years I have become more and more burdened because I find a strong tendency among older pastors to take the fan in their hands. I am told by some that they no longer allow tongues in prayer in public meetings. They will not have the "camp meeting style" of singing and shouting and clapping of hands in their churches. I find many churches where there is never any sign of a truly Pentecostal manifestation. They are afraid of manifestations in the "flesh," and so they conduct the whole meeting "in the flesh," but decently and in order. In such meetings I feel as I do in a home where there are no children, no babies that cry. Everybody behaves perfectly, but it is so dull and so monotonous. Babies and children always do the unexpected. What are we doing with our spiritual babies? Where do we train them? In the basement? Will they ever learn that they belong to the family...the church?

Then again I come to other churches which give me concern. There is no recognition of wheat and there is a premium on chaff— loud talking, shouting and singing for an hour. Everybody is speaking in tongues but there is never any interpretation. It is Pentecostal indeed, but still in the chaff stage—babies crying, children tumbling. It looks bad when adults act like children. Some must come to maturity. There must be tongues with interpretation and there must be prophecy and other manifestations. In such churches I plead that they invite the Baptizer to bring in His fan and then give them a baptism of fire. I have seen too many shouting Christians go to sleep when the Word is preached. They live on "milk" and choke on the "meat" of the Word.

"For when for the time ye ought to be teachers, ye have need that one teach you again which be the first principles of the oracles of God; and are become such as have need of milk, and not of strong meat. For every one that useth milk is unskilful in the word of righteousness: for he is a babe. But strong meat belongeth to them that are of full age, even those who by reason of use have their senses exercised to discern both good and evil" (Heb. 5:12–14).

PENTECOST : FORGOTTEN FESTIVAL

This article was written by the Rev. John Garrett, Director of the Department of Information, World Council of Churches, Geneva, Switzerland. He is a Congregational minister whose home is in Australia.

The Christian feast of Pentecost will be observed this year on June 5. It is an appropriate time for us to ask ourselves if we as Christians have the dynamic experience today which characterized the Church of which we read in the Acts of the Apostles.

Perhaps we of the older denominations should ask ourselves, "Why are the Pentecostal churches thriving?" Some people say it is because they specialize in popular music and are not afraid to let their hair down. The worshippers feel at home because they can forget to be respectable and just enjoy themselves. There are many ways of explaining why some denominations grow and thrive all over the world; but no explanation is good enough if it leaves out their stress on the Holy Spirit and the coming of the Spirit on the assembled disciples. Such people are dynamic, missionary. A real Christian is identifiable partly by his joy, controlled excitement, and missionary concern. Is it not true that since Pentecost every Christian is called to be a "Pentecostalist"?

What happened at Pentecost? Fifty days after the Easter appearance of Christ, an international group of followers of Jesus met in Jerusalem. They were in low spirits; they had been waiting around for something to turn up. It did.

As they sat together and prayed, God came among them. Describing it afterwards, they spoke of wind and fire and the power of speech. They were like Elijah, who had run away from his responsibilities into the desert. God had come to him like a gale that broke up the boulders, like a fire that burned out what was

107

useless, like a "still small voice" that gave him power to speak to his contemporaries and yet remain calm within.

All this happened again in the Jerusalem episode. God the Spirit, who visits man and gives him uncanny strength through all the Old Testament story, came in Jerusalem to the first followers of Jesus Christ. They had been either good, solid, churchgoing Jews or polite inquiring foreigners who wanted to know more about the Jewish religion and the Law of Moses.

The whole group, those who took the God of Abraham as a naturally available and favorable aid to living, and the others who thought of this God of the Jews as inviting them to become Jews themselves, suddenly met God direct. God came to them and gave them the possibility of understanding other men, speaking other languages and becoming articulate prophets like Elijah. The whole crowd, mostly lay Christians, suddenly recognized that the Spirit of God was alive in their local congregation and that things were going to happen as they had never happened before.

We are the same. Just think for a moment of our conventional, steady ways. We all troop into church on Sunday hoping for something to happen. God has provided the minister and the building. We treat them as permanently available public installations, to which we contribute and from which we receive stated services.

The Spirit? Do we think of the Spirit as Him, as God, the judging, purifying maker of our lives who destroys evil, and therefore cannot tolerate us as we are—self-important, self-satisfied, self-absorbed? Or are we like many twentieth-century Christians for whom the Spirit means trying to be good, sweet, true and reliable—"spreading the spirit of Jesus"?

The energy of God that came at Pentecost is quite different from the effort of "good Christians" to do their best every day. A church of "do gooders" is inclined to try to save itself by its own efforts. A church that takes Pentecost seriously knows that it must wait for God himself to change it from a church of Pharisees into a church of Christian witnesses.

What is a witness? He is a man who says, "I saw this happen." The early disciples said: "Christ was murdered by our hostility to God. We saw it happen. We are guilty. Christ was dead, but He is risen and has come to us, the guilty people, to say that we are forgiven and that we must give all we have and are to serve Him. Christ is alive. He is the man God has designated to gather the whole world and all nations back into the Father's home. Christ has sent us the Spirit so that we shall never be tired any more when we serve Him; so that we can receive 'power from on high' to give all our money, our time, our training, our future to Him—and to nobody else."

It may be that the Pentecostals have understood this sometimes better than some others. Is it not possible that they have a central truth of the Christian religion at the heart of their success story? In any case, Pentecost is a time for Christians to become once more the revolutionary members of a dynamic society. Jesus Christ came to turn those who are "conformed to this world" into people who would turn "the world upside down." When whole congregations as conformist as Peter or as self-righteous as Paul become as revolutionary as they were, established customs are in for a shock; and men will learn again that the Holy Spirit is not just light, but a fire that is hard to put out!

(First published in 1959)

A REMARKABLE DOCUMENT

"A Pentecostal could hardly have written a better outline on the ministry gifts," was my first exclamation when I read the little Prayer Bulletin published by the World Council of Churches and drafted by the Commission on Faith and Order.

Week of Prayer for Christian Unity — 1960

To the church of God which is at Corinth...

My congregation is a manifestation of the universal Church in this place.

My congregation is a diversity of different members with different spiritual gifts.

My congregation is a unity in which this diversity is bound together in an organic whole for the common good.

My congregation is an ecumenical microcosm which in its unified diversity shows forth the essential oneness of the Church of Christ and identifies it with "all those who in every place call on the name of our Lord Jesus Christ," whether in the congregation around the corner or at the ends of the earth.

This leaflet, based on I Corinthians 12, especially verses 27 and 28, has as its general theme "The Unity of the Local Congregation in the Unity of the Universal Church." It is designed to help local congregations come to a fresh understanding of themselves in terms of Christian unity, and through this of their ecumenical character and vocation as a manifestation of the one Body of Christ. For Christian unity is not something remote and far away. The local church brings together in one corporate fellowship different members with a variety of gifts and in so doing it experiences the joys and satisfactions as well as the tensions and frustrations which are the growing pains of the Church realizing its unity "as the whole body nourished and knit together through its joints and ligaments grows with a growth that is from God" (Col. 2:19).

Since the last Week of Prayer for Christian Unity it has again become painfully evident that the various calls to prayer have behind them greatly different understandings of the nature of Christian unity. It is also clear that the more Christians come to know one another the more conscious they become of their differences. Nevertheless, there is on all sides a growing conviction that the unity of the Church of Christ is God's will and that He is working to bring it about. That is why, despite the different ideas of unity which lie behind them, it is fruitful to offer up all of our various prayers for Christian unity together at one time: we all know that God hears and answers the prayers of all according to His own will and plan. In this confidence we call upon Christians in all churches to join in prayer for Christian unity during the week of January 18–25.

Commission on Faith and Order

WORLD COUNCIL OF CHURCHES

Week of Prayer for Christian Unity

Theme: THE UNITY OF THE LOCAL CONGREGATION
IN THE UNITY OF THE UNIVERSAL CHURCH

First Day

> *And God has appointed in the church. . .apostles.*
> Read Ephesians 2:19–22 (also I Samuel 3).

As you pray think of the particular local congregation of which you are a member in your own country and generation; in the light of verses 21 and 22 reflect on the early Church and its origin in the witness of those who saw Jesus and testified to His resurrection:

—on the Apostles as foundations of the Church, a source and strength of church unity and the forerunners of the Christian mission

—on the spiritual community of believers from that day to this as fellow-members of the household of God and fellow-citizens with all the saints

—on the need for obedience to God's call, not only for an apostolic vocation but for any Christian witness in the world.

As you pray remember that you are a member of the whole Body of Christ and in particular consider the common apostolic tradition belonging to all churches which binds them together and leads them out into the world.

Let us pray: Almighty God, who hast founded Thy Church upon the witness of the Apostles and Prophets; make, we beseech Thee, their witness living and powerful in our midst also, and grant us Thy grace, that through the teaching of Thy holy Apostles we may be joined together in the unity of the faith, and built up into a holy temple, so that we may be fellow-citizens with all Thy saints. *Amen.*

Second Day

> *And God has appointed in the church...prophets.*
> Read II Peter 1:19–21 (also Jeremiah 20:7–9, 11).

As you pray think of these verses and how the Word of God does not come from human reason but from God's creative Spirit in man:

—how a Spirit-filled understanding brings true light into the world's darkness

—how all prophetic utterance is to enlighten individuals, congregations, and nations, as men listen, hear, and heed the divine Word

—how discernment is needed to distinguish between true and false prophets.

As you pray remember that you are a member of the whole Body of Christ and in particular reflect on the prophetic role of the ecumenical movement in drawing the churches together in renewal for unity, witness, and service.

Let us pray: Visit, O Lord, Thy Church with Thy grace, and enlighten it through the truth of Thy Gospel, which Thou hast imparted to us through Thy holy messengers; awaken our minds that they may hear Thy Word and be obedient to Thy will; enshrine Thy power in the words of Thy messengers and thus enlighten the hearts of Thy faithful people. *Amen*

Third Day

> *And God has appointed in the church. . .teachers.*
> Read II Timothy 3: 14–17 (also Deuteronomy 6: 6–9).

As you pray think of learning and teaching as the transmitting and receiving of mysteries entrusted to us by God:
—of abiding in what you have learned
—of honoring and loving your teachers who fostered faith by helping you to fathom the realms of truth
—of the home and family as the first place of teaching and learning
—of youth as the time of learning and the power of God to renew our youth so that we can continue to learn
—of teaching as life-giving through the creativeness of the Word
—of biblical truth as the ground and aim of all Christian education.

As you pray remember you are a member of the whole Body of Christ and in particular reflect on the Bible as the common textbook of all Christians.

Let us pray: Almighty God, who hast entrusted Thy saving truth unto men, that they may teach it to others; we pray Thee ever to send true shepherds and teachers to prepare and instruct Thy Church and make it into Thy people. Bless, we beseech Thee, the work of all who teach Thy truth throughout Thy holy Church, that we may all be brought to the faith and saved through Thy Gospel. *Amen*.

Fourth Day

> *And God has appointed in the church. . .miracle workers.*
> Read St. Mark 16: 14–18 (also Isaiah 61: 1–3).

As you pray for the renewal of the Church and the recovery of its wholeness think of the God-given unity of soul and body of the spiritual and the material:

—of God's power to create out of nothing and of His power to make all things new both in the Church and in the world

—of all things being possible with God and the unwillingness to believe as the greatest spiritual danger

—of the need of the new and miraculous for the healthy life of the Church.

As you pray remember that you are a member of the whole Body of Christ and in particular consider the place of new gifts of the Spirit and new ministries in the life of the Church as it is renewed in wholeness and unity.

Let us pray: O God of unchangeable power and eternal light, look favorably on Thy whole Church, that wonderful and sacred mystery; and by the operation of Thy providence, carry out the work of man's salvation; and let the whole world feel and see that things which were cast down are being raised up, that those things which had grown old are being made new, and that all things are returning to perfection through Him from whom they took their origin, even through our Lord Jesus Christ. *Amen.*

Fifth Day

> *And God has appointed in the church. . .healers.*
> Read James 5: 13–16 (also Jeremiah 17: 13–15).

As you pray concentrate on the meaning of these verses in your particular situation:

—on Christ's command to His disciples both to preach and heal

—on the calling of church members to minister to the sick of the community, giving not only pastoral but bodily care

—on earnestly engaging in intercessory prayer and really seeking to share in the healing process

—on anointing of the sick both sacramentally and by acts of mercy, and inwardly by the fellowship of love and prayer

—on Christ's concern for the whole man spiritual and physical.

As you pray also remember that you are a member of the whole Body of Christ and in particular reflect on the acts of healing done by Christians together through various organizations and institutions.

Let us pray: Lord, have mercy on us in the misery of our sin and in the suffering of all sinners. May Thy love descend upon all the homes which wait for Thy mercy. Visit also with Thy love all those who do not know Thy mercy; help the lonely, the tempted, the afflicted, the crushed, and all who must face death. *Amen.*

Sixth Day

> *And God has appointed in the church . . . helpers.*
> Read Colossians 3: 12–16 (also Isaiah 17: 10–12).

As you pray think of the responsibility which each member of the Christian fellowship bears for every other member:

—of the fellowship of worship in confession and absolution in praise and song, as a help rather than a hindrance for the common life, and a means of uniting rather than separating us

—of service in and to the world as an expression of the service of worship of the congregation in the church.

As you pray remember that you are a member of the whole Body of Christ and in particular consider the service of the laity in the life and work of the Church, and as one people of God in the world, and especially of the help rendered through inter church aid and service to refugees as a sign of the unity of Christ's Body, in which the members all suffer and rejoice together and care for one another.

Let us pray: Merciful Father, awaken us, we pray Thee, to true love of our brethren, that we may be ready and willing to succour and support all who are in difficulty or suffering whether far or near; that we may serve our neighbors to the utmost of our power, and have open hearts and outstretched hands to all who suffer throughout the world, so that we may witness to Thy love, and the message of Thy Gospel may thus be strengthened. *Amen.*

Seventh Day

> *And God has appointed in the church... leaders.*
> Read Acts 20: 28 (also Ezekiel 34: 11–16).

As you pray remember the ministry, clerical and lay:
—the episcopal and priestly ministry
—the preaching and pastoral ministry
—the evangelistic and teaching ministry
—the responsibility of all leaders for sound doctrine
—the application of the Word of God in the life and activity of the congregation and community.

As you pray remember that you are a member of the whole Body of Christ and in particular reflect on the need for manifestations of unity through church organizations—denominational boards, church synods, confessional alliances, local and national councils of churches, and especially for the World Council of Churches, its staff, officers, and members of its committees.

Let us pray: Almighty and everlasting God, who alone canst perform miracles and givest us more than we can ask or understand; pour the grace of Thy Holy Spirit upon all Thy servants and the communities in their care; bind both clergy and people together in true love, that they may both serve and be a blessing to one another. *Amen.*

Eighth Day

> *And God has appointed in the church... speakers in*
> *tongues and interpreters.*
> Read Acts 2: 4–11 (also Genesis 40: 5–8).

As you pray think of the meaning of these verses as they apply to your own particular congregation, remembering the significance of the unusual and extraordinary in the Christian Church as opposed to the normal and mediocre:
—of the witness which does not come only from the intellect and transcends the understanding of man
—of the need for interpretation and expression as well as for language that can be understood everywhere and by all
—of "speakers in tongues" who continually challenge and

disturb the Church which all too easily becomes complacent and self-satisfied and contented to remain as it is.

As you pray remember that you are a member of the whole Body of Christ and reflect on the place within the Body of those individuals and groups which do not fit easily or comfortably into the present ecclesiastical and ecumenical patterns.

Let us pray: Almighty God, who dost teach the hearts of Thy faithful people by sending to them the light of Thy Holy Spirit; grant us by the same Spirit to have a right judgment in all things, and evermore to rejoice in His holy comfort, through Jesus Christ our Lord. *Amen.*

David J. du Plessis

Please add me to your prayer list.

CONCLUSION

In the previous section on pages 117 and 118 the Commission n Faith and Order of the World Council of Churches invites all ） "remember the significance of the *unusual and extraordinary* ą the Christian Church as opposed to the normal and mediocre," ąd then reminds us that "speakers in tongues" continually chalɔnge and disturb the Church which all too easily becomes comąacent and self-satisfied and content to remain as it is.

I am delighted to inform readers that this is no idle talk ąsofar as the ministry is concerned in constituent bodies of the ⁊orld Council. During the past five years I have personally enɔyed the fellowship of scores of Episcopal, Lutheran, Presbyɔrian, Methodist, Reformed, Congregational, Baptist, and other ąurchmen who have received a baptism in the Holy Spirit with ąe confirmation of "tongues" and the manifestation of all the ⁊fts of the Spirit.

While I have had fellowship with scores, there are hundreds ⁊ whom I have heard but have not met. This number is increasąg at an amazing pace. In the summer of 1961 it was my priviɔge to pray with many serious seekers in the ministry who are ⁊nvinced they need this enduement with power, and I have seen ąe Spirit fall upon them as upon the Apostles in the Book of Acts, ąd upon the Pentecostals during the last half century. Many ɔceived in their private devotions after I had opened the Scripąres to them. Then they were able to minister to others. In some ɔry recent cases such brethren were able to lead their colleagues ąto a truly Pentecostal experience, and others have ministered ） their own members in prayer groups that have been intercedąg with God for a Holy Spirit revival and the renewal of the ąurch in this age.

> "Glory, glory, hallelujah!
> His truth is marching on."

A FURTHER CONCLUSION

The first printing of this book appeared in 1960. A second printing was called for in 1962. The reception of the message and its effect upon readers far exceeded my fondest dreams. In 1961 I began to work on another book dealing more fully with the person and work of the Holy Spirit. This is still in its first manuscript form. Constant travel and ministry has not allowed me time enough to complete the work.

In the meantime the Lord has blessed in such unexpected ways that the ministry has taken on deeper and wider dimensions than I had thought possible. It is now evident that the second book is not "ripe" for publication and will have to be completely rewritten.

The urgent and insistant call for more teaching on the baptism in the Spirit and on the issue of Glossolalia has persuaded me to take care of this need by adding a few chapters and rearranging others in this printing of *The Spirit Bade Me Go*. Indeed, I can say, the Spirit bade me *write*. I realize that these writings may not be considered profound studies, but I only seek to teach a few simple truths. The truth is always liberating.

Judging from the most recent writings in the religious press in both magazines and books, one cannot help but notice that the general interest in the Holy Spirit and His manifestations in the Church is increasing at such a pace that it has become impossible to keep track of this 20th century renewal of the Church.

The wind bloweth where it listeth. In the older churches and the younger churches, in home churches and foreign churches, in Roman Catholic, Orthodox, Protestant and Pentecostal churches, things are happening that can be understood only in the light of the eschatological fulfillment of Joel 2. God is pouring of His Spirit upon all flesh. It seems all churches are opening their windows and doors to the refreshing breezes of spiritual renewal.

From the beginning of 1961 up to the present time I have had the privilege of seeing hundreds of ministers and missionaries receiving the baptism in the Holy Spirit. Hundreds more that I have not seen have written about their encounter with Christ the Baptizer. During these last three years students in seminaries, universities and colleges have begun to accept the baptism in the Spirit. There is no mass movement, but thank God, it is both international and inter-denominational.

I trust and pray that the third printing of this book will receive an even warmer reception than the first two. I hope it will help to spread the good news and cause waves of revival to roll ever further and deeper in all churches.

David J. du Plessis

A BRIEF LIFE SKETCH OF THE WRITER

Born February 7, 1905, in South Africa.

A descendant of the French Huguenots.

Converted at an early age and baptized in the Holy Spirit in 1918.

Married to Anna Cornelia Jacobs August 13, 1927. One daughter and five sons were born to this marriage.

Ordained to the ministry in 1928 by the Apostolic Faith Mission of South Africa.

Served as evangelist, pastor, youth leader, Sunday school director, chief editor, and general secretary of the mission from 1928 to 1948.

Resident in the U.S.A. since 1949. Served as lecturer in Lee College, Church of God, Cleveland, Tenn., 1949 and 1950. In 1955 his ordination papers were transferred from South Africa to the Assemblies of God, U.S.A.

Attended the First Pentecostal World Conference in 1947 in Zurich, Switzerland.

Served as secretary and organized the Second Pentecostal World Conference in Paris, France, 1949; and the Third Pentecostal World Conference in London, England, 1952. Then again the Fifth Pentecostal World Conference, 1958, in Toronto, Canada.

Attended the Sixth Pentecostal World Conference, May 1961, Jerusalem.

Attended the meetings of the International Missionary Council at Willingen, Germany, in 1952, as observer. Served as special consultant of the International Missionary Council in Ghana, West Africa, in 1958.

Served on the staff of the Second Assembly of the World Council of Churches during the 1954 meetings at Evanston. Attended the Third Assembly of the World Council of Churches, New Delhi, 1961, as Pentecostal observer.

Attended the World Assembly of the Presbyterian and Reformed World Alliance at Princeton, N. J., in 1954. Served as Pentecostal Fraternal delegate to the 18th General Council of the Presbyterian World Alliance at Sao Paulo, Brazil, in 1959.

During 1959, lectured on Pentecostal Issues at Princeton Seminary (Missions Lectures). Also at Evangelical Congregational School of Theology, Myertstown, Pa.; Yale Divinity School, New Haven, Conn.; Union Theological Seminary, New York; The Ecumenical Institute of the World Council of Churches at Chateau de Bossey in Switzerland, and Perkins School of Theology, Southern Methodist University, Dallas.

During 1960, participated in the Consultation on Evangelism of the WCC at the Ecumenical Institute in Switzerland; and in the Commission of Faith and Order at St. Andrews University in Scotland.

During 1961 lectured in British Columbia University in Vancouver, B.C.; Colgates Rochester School of Divinity, Rochester, N. Y.; and The Ecumenical Institute of the United Presbyterian Church at Stony Point, N. Y.

Has preached in 45 countries of the world and hopes to reach others soon.

Feels called to labor for better understanding and closer fellowship between Pentecostal movements, and to bring the Pentecostal message and blessing into the ranks of all Christian churches.

Always serves freely as the Lord supplies for travel and for family. Not sponsored or salaried by any one source.